The psychology of social issues

Employment and unemployment

The psychology of social issues

This series is concerned with the application of social psychology to issues of contemporary social importance. It is inspired by the belief that academic social psychology has for too long operated at a level of theory and research that has effectively denied its most interesting ideas and results to the general reader, and it aims specifically to remedy this. Books included in the series will be short, non-technical, and accessibly written. They will survey the relevant research in social psychology and other disciplines, and authors will also be encouraged to develop their own ideas – excitingly where possible and controversially where necessary.

Publisher's note. Henri Tajfel was the founding editor of this series, and its chief inspiration. He died while this book was still in production, but his direct or indirect influence will be felt and reflected in all forthcoming titles.

Employment and unemployment

A social-psychological analysis

MARIE JAHODA

CAMBRIDGE UNIVERSITY PRESS

Cambridge

London New York New Rochelle

Melbourne Sydney

Published by the Press Syndicate of the University of Cambridge
The Pitt Building, Trumpington Street, Cambridge CB2 1RP
32 East 57th Street, New York, NY 10022, USA
296 Beaconsfield Parade, Middle Park, Melbourne 3206, Australia

First published 1982

Printed in Great Britain at the University Press, Cambridge

Library of Congress catalogue card number: 82-4165

British Library Cataloguing in Publication Data

Jahoda, Marie
Employment and unemployment: a social-psychological analysis. –
(The psychology of social issues)
1. Unemployment
I. Title   II. Series
331.13'7   HD5706
ISBN 0 521 24294 0 hard covers
ISBN 0 521 28586 0 paperback

Contents

Acknowledgements

This book is only to a small extent based on my own empirical work; it relies heavily on that of other social psychologists, much more numerous than could be named in the following pages, with whom I share a lifelong preoccupation with the social and psychological issues in employment and unemployment. I am deeply indebted to this invisible community of people – even those with whom I disagree – whose unceasing efforts to enlarge knowledge about one of the crucial problems of our times deserve a more prominent place in the debate about work and its future than has been accorded them so far.

One reason for this relative neglect of the contributions social psychologists have made to the understanding of the world in which we live is the inaccessibility to a wider audience of their technical reports. I am grateful to Henri Tajfel and Jeremy Mynott, who as editor and publisher, respectively, conceived the idea for this series of publications, for having invited me to participate in this effort to make the work of social psychologists more widely known.

In writing this book I have freely drawn on my previous publications, often verbatim, without burdening the text with the corresponding references. If this is legitimate where I alone am concerned, it disguises the contributions that others have made to my knowledge and views. I want to thank particularly Howard Rush with whom I have previously worked and published on matters dealt with in these pages. He has read a draft of each chapter in this book and his comments and criticisms have invariably helped me to greater clarity.

Austen Albu has regarded the production of this book as a continuation of decades of shared concern and conversation about employment and unemployment. His critical realism has deeply influenced me. His questioning of every phrase and comma has added to the spice of life; it also improved the text.

Acknowledgements

During the production of this book I was employed as a part-time consultant at the Science Policy Research Unit at the University of Sussex. This stimulating assignment has enriched my knowledge and broadened my outlook.

I am grateful to Linda Gardiner who typed the manuscript and supported me throughout with her unflagging competence and cheerfulness.

Keymer   M.J.
September 1981

1

Introduction

Throughout human history the overwhelming majority of people have worked for their living. They still do, but now a question-mark hangs over the future of work in the Western world. Unemployment rates are rising in industrialised countries in a world-wide recession. A new international division of labour eliminates some employment opportunities in the rich world; this rich world must therefore concentrate on new technologies which, in turn, have the potential of replacing the work of human beings and still have to demonstrate their power of creating new jobs for all.

There are some who expect that the issue of unemployment will be reduced to manageable proportions once the world recession eases. There are others who point to the probably irreversible change in the international division of labour and its implications for the reduction in the number of jobs in the rich world. To survive economically technological innovation becomes imperative; by the same token the most widely feared and advocated new technology – microprocessors – eliminates many jobs. In this double bind even technological optimists do not offer a solution for unemployment in the near future though they paint a glowing picture of more distant possibilities. According to temperament they either speak of a leisure society in which work will be unnecessary for many while inherently interesting for a few or, more soberly, they point to the enormous changes in the nature and number of jobs that have followed in the past changes in the structure of the economy or the introduction of new technologies. During the last hundred years or so millions of jobs were lost in agriculture and domestic services but new ones emerged in factories. Henry Ford's labour-saving invention of the conveyor belt created in the end more jobs, not fewer. Such optimists recall the automation debates in the fifties of this century, when equally dire predictions of structural unemployment were disproved by subsequent events.

Whether or not history will repeat itself only the twenty-first century will reveal. For the less distant future in the United Kingdom and elsewhere unemployment will most likely present a major social problem in the 1980s. In economic terms it imposes an enormous burden. One recent estimate of the economic cost of unemployment to the U.K. government, taking into account the costs of benefits, their administration, employment services and the loss in income and insurance contributions, arrives at a figure of over £4,000 million (Showler and Sinfield, 1981, p. 52). Another estimate emerges with a figure of more than £5,000 million (Samuel Brittan, 1981), and the costs are rising with the rising number of unemployed. The economic cost to the individual unemployed is, according to the same sources, on the average a reduction of about 50% of disposable income. Such a reduction imposes problems whatever the level of income at which it occurs. When it hits the growing number of long-term unemployed who depend on supplementary benefits, having exhausted their unemployment insurance, and who are disproportionately composed of the lowest paid in previous employment, the economic hardship is indeed severe.

The public debate about unemployment, divided though it is about causes and prospects, is virtually unanimous in its restriction to macro- and micro-economic issues, taking their social and psychological implications so much for granted that economic goals lose their character as means and become ends in themselves. There is, of course, no question about the overwhelming importance of the economic state of affairs both for the country at large and for its unemployed; but equally there is no question that the ultimate criterion by which economic strategies must be judged is not trade balances or Gross National Product but the quality of life people experience who are affected by such strategies. Being employed or unemployed is a major component of this quality.

Quality of life is an elusive concept that defies exact measurement. Its many components – work or its absence, economic circumstances, psychological predisposition, personal relations, health, the social climate and fate – are analytically separate though unified in experience where they interact in an inextricable manner. In line with the

2

materialism of our culture the most easily measurable aspect, economic circumstances, is often taken as the single indicator of quality of life; perhaps justifiably so where deprivation in economic terms is severe. In this country many of the long-term unemployed live below the poverty-line, as do other large families where the main earner of the family is disabled or on very low wages. But to leave it at that amounts to a very one-sided view of what human beings need to make sense out of their lives. Bread – yes; but not only and more than circuses.

This book is an attempt to present to a wider public the contribution of social psychology to the understanding of employment and unemployment. The size of this contribution is enormous; its availability to an audience outside the community of social psychologists is very limited. Most of the relevant ideas and research results are published in technical journals where there is legitimately much emphasis on details of method and where the use of established scientific terminology must be taken for granted. By this same token, however, this vast technical literature fails to enter the wider public debate about work.

I have tried to avoid both jargon and oversimplification in the conviction that the massive research effort of social psychologists in this field deserves to be more widely known than it currently is, even though it does not offer solutions to the many problems the topic implies. Indeed, one would be rightly suspicious if any discipline pretended to have *the* answer to issues that by their nature demand not only considerations from other disciplines – economics, political science, sociology, history – but above all practical political commitment. Just because we live in a period in which economic thought and economic necessities dominate public policy it is important to insist that other dimensions be considered too; all the more so because economic thought rests inevitably on some tacit assumptions about what people want, need and value. While some of the great economists have on occasion made their psychological views explicit – Adam Smith, Karl Marx, Maynard Keynes, for example – they remain personal convictions untested by systematic study. Social psychology can provide some of the missing links although it is no substitute for political commitment.

That unemployment is economically 'bad' is beyond question, both for the collectivity and for the individual. To assess its other human consequences requires a comparison with the human consequences of employment. For if employment has lost its meaning for many, as the ever-growing literature on alienation asserts, unemployment would indeed be an economic issue only. While public attention is understandably concentrated on the increasing rates of unemployment, its consequences cannot be understood in isolation from the conditions under which the vast majority of the population make their living.

Any presentation of what is systematically known about employment and unemployment must inevitably be selective. During this century a truly staggering amount of empirical work on these matters has accumulated that defies comprehensive coverage. A recent bibliography, for example, restricted to the period 1970–1977 and to a limited topic – work organisation – lists over 1,100 items (Brake, 1978). Understandably, nobody has tried to produce a comprehensive bibliography and nobody can any longer claim to be on top of the literature in this rich, vital and sprawling field of study. A choice has to be made, even within the imposed limitation of incomplete knowledge.

One possibility for deliberate selection would be a concentration on recent research, justified by the indubitable fact that research methods have increased in sophistication to an extraordinary extent in the second half of this century. But there are weighty counter-arguments. While the improvement in methodology is all to the good, of course, such a choice would ignore a problem peculiar to the social sciences. In the natural sciences, which deal with phenomena immune to historical changes, if more sophisticated methods yield different results they are as a rule assumed to be more valid than earlier findings. No such assumption is possible in the social sciences. Not only methods change, but also people and history; what complicates the issue is that they do not keep step with the same clock. To decide whether yesterday's findings are valid for today, let alone for tomorrow, is a difficult matter. Perhaps the earlier methods were too crude; perhaps people's values have changed; or perhaps the conditions have changed under which they are now employed or unemployed. But to ignore earlier findings would cut off social psychology from one of its central tasks: to contribute to the understanding of social change.

Many text-books of industrial psychology have recognised the need for a historical dimension, but have dealt with it in terms of the history of research rather than in terms of social change. So it has become customary to present the topic starting early in the century with Taylorism and its emphasis on efficiency and productivity (curiously acclaimed by Lenin in 1919), proceeding to the Hawthorne studies and the human relations approach, from there to group-dynamics, to the socio-technical systems approach of the Tavistock Institute, to more recent concern with job enrichment and enlargement and to what West German social scientists call the humanisation of work.

This may be an adequate description of the sequence of dominant research interests; it is certainly not a sequence of the problems in the real world of work. Efficiency, productivity, human relations and the nature of jobs are issues as urgent now as they were when they preoccupied researchers or failed to do so.

Neither a concentration on unemployment alone nor on the most recent research literature nor on a historical review of dominant research interests determines, therefore, the selection of material in the following presentation. The choice, in as far as it is deliberate and not the result of inevitably limited knowledge, is in favour of studies that illuminate the complexity of human experiences in daily life. This excludes laboratory studies as much as a discussion of a variety of theories that have guided such research in recent decades, important though they are for the advancement of a single discipline. These exclusions require a brief justification.

Some laboratory experiments – for example on conformity, obedience to authority, communication patterns in small groups or minimal conditions for group formation – have an obvious relevance for thinking about the world of work. But the transfer of results from experimentally contrived situations to the complexities of experience outside the laboratory is still so tenuous a matter that notwithstanding some splendid achievements in experimental social psychology, its power to illuminate experience appears to be limited.

Much the same holds true for theories. There is no single theory that encompasses the full richness of empirical results, nor that deals satisfactorily with the occasionally contradictory findings. Many of the relevant studies are frankly atheoretical; others are based on diverse theories about human behaviour and experience that are in principle incompatible with each other, because they are designed to provide explanations for different types of phenomena. A theory designed to explain the physiological concomitants of work or unemployment cannot encompass data on their subjective meaning; a theory concerned with social comparisons cannot deal with the phenomena of intra-psychic conflict; a theory about alienation as a consequence of the division of labour is unsuitable for explaining individual differences in attitudes to work. Every theory inevitably selects limited aspects out of the vast reservoir of behaviour and experience and uses appropriate concepts, units of analysis and methods within its restricted scope of convenience; the very appropriateness for one purpose makes it inappropriate for another. This is as it must be if theoretical thought is to advance; by the same token it deprives an approach to the study of work of that most useful function of a theory, which is to summarise available knowledge. To be sure there are some systems of thought, often misclassified as theories, that provide a unifying point of view for the study of any social phenomenon: neo-Marxism is one, neo-conservatism another. They are world views rather than theories, because they rest on *a priori* value assumptions that cannot be verified or falsified by reference to the real world. There is a price to be paid for these exclusions; the rigour of causal explanations will have to be replaced by descriptions and indications of circular causalities. I see no way of avoiding it.

The empirical literature from various disciplines in the social sciences, on which this book is based, deals as a rule with unemployment and employment, not with work or its absence. The reasons for keeping these terms distinct are set out in the next chapter.

There then follows an attempt to present a historical background for the current situation. Chapter 3 describes the findings from studies of the social-psychological consequences of unemployment conducted during the great depression of the 1930s in various countries. The intention in that chapter is to suggest broad categories of experience that occurred with unemployment as a basis for comparison with the present. Because of this intention two studies that had concentrated on many dimensions of this multi-faceted experience are extensively used: the study of Marienthal, a one-factory village in Austria that was almost totally unemployed when the factory closed in 1929 (Jahoda, Lazarsfeld and Zeisel, 1933), and a study of unemployed men who lived among others still employed in Greenwich, England (Bakke, 1933).

The following chapter deals first with the enormous social changes that have taken place in the last half-century that can be assumed to have affected the current experiences of both unemployment and employment, and then looks at empirical evidence to test the justification of such assumptions. As is to be expected this evidence is not always conclusive and its interpretation far from unanimous. It emerges that it is easier to generalise about the experience of unemployment than of employment with its larger variability.

In Chapter 5, therefore, the reality of current employment is further examined, particularly with emphasis on the results of numerous efforts to improve conditions, their successes and their failures. It will not come as a surprise to the informed reader that notwithstanding the tragedy of mass unemployment, there is also tragedy in some forms of modern employment, not all of it inevitable, however.

In the last chapter there is a summary of what appears to me to be the essential contribution of social-psychological thought and research to the understanding of work, employment and unemployment and an effort to apply this to the various alternatives available in the not too distant future.

2

Definitions and their implications

In common parlance as well as in the social science literature, work and employment are often used interchangeably. This conflation of meaning is deeply embedded in our language habits. We speak about work satisfaction or alienation from work, but mean responses to employment; people demonstrate for the right to work when what they want is jobs. A collection of the life stories of the currently unemployed is entitled *Workless* (Marsden and Duff, 1975), another book *The Workless State* (Showler and Sinfield, 1981), yet another *The Collapse of Work* (Jenkins and Sherman, 1979); what is meant in all these cases is the absence of jobs for all who want them. To question the wisdom of such engrained language habits would be pointless without some good conceptual reasons. Granted that in the modern world the two terms are used virtually synonymously, there are such reasons. The *Oxford English Dictionary* lists no less than 39 distinct meanings for the term work, of which holding a job to make a living is only one. The essential communality of all these meanings is action for a purpose or the product of such action. In that sense work is not only an inalienable right (in the sense in which the American Constitution guarantees the inalienable right to the pursuit of happiness) but the very essence of being alive. It is clearly a superordinate notion that includes but is not limited to employment.

Employment or jobs refers to work under contractual arrangements involving material rewards. This definition does not encompass all economically relevant forms of work. Excluded by this narrower conception is not only work performed at different historical periods or in contemporary non-industrialised societies but also forms in industrialised societies: by the self-employed, most housework, work in the 'hidden' economy or voluntary work for social purposes and do-it-yourself activities. All this is work, too.

Economists have as much trouble in distinguishing precisely the many meanings of the term work as other social scientists, even though it is an essential ingredient of their discipline. In 1890 Alfred Marshall proposed this definition: 'We may define labour as an exertion of mind or body undergone partly or wholly with a view to some good other than the pleasure derived directly from work'. This is a broader conception than current language habits imply but it ignores the distinction between employment and other work. While Marshall by implication admits that work can be enjoyable, some modern economists take a sterner view of such activities. It has been suggested, for example, that for purposes of economics every activity should be regarded as work for which it is in principle possible to hire another person with similar qualifications so that the result of the activity remains the same (Hawrylyshyn, 1971). This quite properly excludes watching television or practising a musical instrument; work too, but not in the economic sense. No substitution is possible for such activities. This definition includes housework and the hidden economy, but it rules out of court as externalities the human aspects of gainful employment and, once again, it does not distinguish between holding a job and other forms of economic activity.

There are several reasons why for the purposes of a social-psychological approach to the world of work it is necessary to distinguish clearly between three forms of work: that captured in Marshall's broad definition, employment as regulated by contractual arrangements, and other economic activities not so regulated.

This distinction clarifies at once one aspect of the research literature and of the current debate about the issue: it is employment on which they concentrate, not work. Nonetheless some though not all of these activities outside contractual arrangements make a substantial contribution to the wealth of a nation, although of an unknown proportion. Their inevitable exclusion from official statistics implies that such reports cannot claim to reflect economic conditions comprehensively but present unquestionably an underestimate of economic levels. Only one form of such activities is beginning to attract widespread attention: the hidden economy, which seems to have grown considerably in recent

9

years. The reason for growing concern with this phenomenon is obvious: it implies enormous losses in tax revenue. For France, for example, this loss is estimated to be well over £2,000 million. The human implications are less often commented on, but they are equally obvious: the labour law of the land is powerless in the hidden economy, nor do its participants receive the protection of the trade unions. There is no restriction on working hours, children are involved, apparently particularly in Italy, and exploitation of the weaker among the participants is beyond control. There are indications that in the U.S.A., Canada and West Germany, for example, the manpower for the hidden economy comes to a large extent from people who are employed but engage in second undeclared jobs, even though some registered unemployed also participate. To the extent that jobs are performed behind the back of the tax collector, the phenomenon is an indicator of public morality. By the same token, however, it contradicts the often-made glib diagnosis of our times that people have lost the will to work.

It stands to reason that work in these three categories – under conditions of employment, other activities with an economic purpose (of which the hidden economy is only one aspect) and work done largely for non-economic purposes such as hobbies or children's homework – encompasses activities under vastly differing conditions, eliciting vastly differing satisfactions and frustrations.

It is often assumed that the psychologically constructive aspects of work dominate in activities outside modern conditions of employment, the negative ones in employment where, it is asserted, people have lost their concern for quality, are resistant to technological change, to innovations and labour-saving devices of all kinds as well as being unwilling to do dirty work or keep 'unsocial' hours. There is much current experience to show that this is indeed often the case. As a generalisation, however, these assertions will not hold. Not all is well in the world of employment, but neither is it in the world of work outside. The housewife syndrome of boredom and depression is still a fact of life, and not to be explained by lack of work; housewives certainly welcome as a rule labour-saving devices such as washing machines which reduce the required investment of time and effort to keep a family going. Some people engaged in craft hobbies, however, reject labour-saving devices as do some employed people. Industrial

10

archaeologists wallow in the dirty task of cleaning a waterlogged mill wheel during the 'unsocial' hours of a weekend, activities that they might resent under conditions of employment; nurses, however, who also have to deal with many 'dirty' jobs and night duties are, as a rule, devoted to these activities under conditions of employment. Some self-employed may well long for the relative security of the regularly employed, their circumscribed working hours and reduced responsibility. Retired people often long for the human aspects of employment. Above all, it is the growing number of the unemployed who want jobs, not just work, and not only because of their reduced standard of living.

It follows from the distinctions of three basic forms of work that unemployment should be contrasted with employment, not with work. If empirical research indicates that unemployment interferes with the ability of many to engage in work outside contractual arrangements, this should be regarded as a result needing further explanation, not as a *fiat* by inappropriate definitions.

There are also confusions about the definition of unemployment (Garraty, 1978). The International Labour Office has for decades attempted – unsuccessfully – to establish an internationally acceptable definition; but the legal definitions of unemployment still vary from country to country. In the U.K., for example, the basis for establishing official rates of unemployment are the registrations at local employment offices. In the U.S.A. 'unemployed people comprise all those who did not work during the survey week, who made specific efforts to find a job within the previous four weeks and who were available for work during the survey week' (*Social Trends*, 1980, p. 294).

Sorrentino (1979) has examined the various assumptions underlying official statistics in nine countries and recalculated the published rates on the basis of the definition used in the U.S.A. in order to make international comparisons more meaningful. This painstaking exercise involved inevitably some guesses where comparable data were not available. While the rank order of countries was not changed by adjustment to the U.S. definition, the unemployment rate was; in Great Britain, for example, the official rate was 5.6% in 1976, the adjusted rate 6.4%.

Comparisons between countries can thus not be accurate. In any case, there is general agreement that in every single country the official unemployment rates present only a rough approximation to the actual number of people able and willing to take a job but, at the given moment, without one.

There is a continuing debate about the degree of over- or under-estimate in published data. Where sample surveys are available that elicit self-descriptions of being employed or unemployed they show as a rule severe under-representation of the unemployed in official data. So an Australian study concluded from a probability sample of 9,000 households that the rate of female unemployment was 20.3%; at the same time the Australian Bureau of Statistics estimated this rate as 9% for New South Wales (Council of Social Service of N.S.W., 1978). Similarly, an E.E.C. survey in the nine countries of the community based on personal interviews discovered that among all those who had personally experienced unemployment between 1975 and 1978, 37% had never registered. This proportion was found to be particularly high for Italy (49%) and the U.K. (43%), lowest in Belgium (14%) and West Germany (20%) (European Omnibus, 1978). One factor explaining the discrepancy between official data and survey results is the probability that the latter include people who have given up hope of finding work and have dropped out of the official labour force, but still experience themselves as unemployed. Survey figures have, of course, their own problems of possible distortion. For present purposes I do not assume them to be correct, but conclude only that the experience of unemployment is most probably even more widespread than the increasing official rates in the industrialised world indicate.

There are counter-arguments against this assumption. A large number of the unemployed included in official data find another job after a few weeks and present what is called 'frictional' unemployment. The suggestion has even been made (Wood, 1975, as quoted in Showler and Sinfield, 1981) that short-term unemployment should be excluded from published statistics, as should the 'unemployable', however defined. If such statistical manipulation were performed it would certainly change first impressions of the magnitude of the issue, but would, of course, leave the underlying situation as it is; its seriousness would then be judged by the falling number of job vacancies, and the growing number of redundancies and bankruptcies and of the long-term unemployed. There is some evidence in any case for the U.K. that frictional unemployment has grown less than long-term unemployment and is largely limited to the young in low-skilled jobs.

Even within such limitation official rates are inevitably only crude indicators, aggregating a variety of experiences that vary with individual life circumstances such as age, sex, race, family size and responsibility, skills and, above all, length of unemployment, and with the labour market situation in different localities. No country has yet reached the frighteningly high national rate of unemployment of the great depression – almost a quarter of the labour force. But in places such as the steel-towns in Wales or the North of England, in Detroit and in these and other countries' inner city slums rates have now far exceeded the national average in the thirties.

From a social-psychological point of view one can ignore the differences in legal definition and the consequent differences in enumeration techniques and regard as unemployed all who have not got a job but would like to have one or who when they have no job are dependent on some financial support from whatever source for their livelihood. The first part of this definition excludes the idle rich but includes executives and professionals who though perhaps not dependent on their salaries nevertheless want a job. The second part of the definition includes those who may have adapted to unemployment, are content to live on welfare or family support and no longer want or expect a job.

The foregoing discussion of various definitions of work and unemployment demonstrates that more than pedantry is involved in clarifying the terms used in this book. Having clarified them does not, however, dispense with language habits. Even though all job holders should properly be called employees, in common usage 'employee' carries more prestige than 'worker'. An employee is assumed to be a white-collar worker and to receive a weekly or monthly salary, a blue-collar worker to receive hourly or weekly wages; equally an 'employee' frequently can look forward to annual increments, while a 'worker' cannot but is without 'career' prospects and often at the height of his earning power in his early twenties. It would be less easy to maintain these divisory status differences if our terminology followed the logic of the definitions proposed here. Wherever possible I shall refer to all job holders as employees, albeit without much hope of thereby changing the language habits, let alone the status distinctions.

Definitions in the human sciences are not neutral. They are signposts

13

to the identification of the phenomena that deserve investigation and – wittingly or unwittingly – often imply value judgements about what is tolerable and what intolerable in a civilised society. The definitions adopted here share this lack of neutrality; but it will be evidence for the social and psychological consequences of various forms of employment and unemployment, not just personal conviction, that in the end should justify their adoption.

3

Social and psychological consequences of unemployment in the nineteen-thirties

To adopt a social-psychological perspective requires that the actions and experiences of people be related to the social context in which they occur. This deceptively simple requirement implies both a difficulty and an opportunity for arriving at generalisations about the human consequences of unemployment for the unemployed, particularly when available knowledge based on systematic studies spans half a century, as it does in this case.

The difficulty consists in doubts about the usefulness of the fairly extensive research literature on unemployment that accumulated during the depression in the thirties for illuminating the situation in the eighties. Some modern commentators are untouched by such doubts and assume that what was true then is true now. They may well be right, but for the wrong reasons of a blind assumption. Too much has changed both in the social climate and in the aspirations, values, hopes and fears, needs and beliefs of the population in the last fifty years for leaving it at that. If one adds the further complication that most of the earlier studies of unemployment used relatively unsophisticated methods of enquiry, a case could actually be made for ignoring them completely.

Doing so, however, would be tantamount to missing the opportunity of contributing to a deeper understanding of the impact of unemployment. If it were found that modern unemployment was psychologically less disturbing now than in the past one would conclude that the standard of living to which the unemployed were then reduced – subsistence level and often below – had a greater weight in shaping their experiences than the absence of a job, which would emerge as a matter of secondary importance. If, on the other hand, the modern unemployed showed similar psychological disturbances under unquestionably better living conditions than in the past, economic deprivation would count for less, the absence of employment for more in explaining their experiences. By implication either finding would throw some light on the meaning of work in the modern world. This is why it is worth summarising, with due caution about methodological shortcomings, the results from studies of the impact of unemployment in the thirties, a period when it meant, as a rule, living in severe poverty. It should be noted, however, that poverty has always had other causes too – a fact now sometimes overlooked. As early as 1899 Rowntree found in his famous study of poverty in York that in 52% of families in poverty the main earner had a regular job but on insufficient wages. In only 2% of cases was poverty due to unemployment (quoted in Hyman, 1979, p. 297).

Since the institution of workhouses under the Poor Laws in the reign of Elizabeth I some public provision has been available for those in need: the improvident, the workshy, the mentally or physically disabled, deserted wives with children *and* those who could not find paid employment. But so harsh were the living conditions in these workhouses, so defaming the stigma attached to them that through the centuries many preferred begging to dependence on such public charity. Only in this century, in 1911, were those willing to work but not able to find employment clearly distinguished from the rest of the poor. The original insurance scheme in the U.K. was limited to building, engineering and ship-building, three trades in which employment opportunities fluctuated with some regularity, a situation clearly independent of the workers' willingness to take a job. During the First World War munitions workers were included and after it ex-servicemen. In 1920 the scheme was extended to cover the vast majority of those in employment. At the time of the short-lived post-war boom nobody expected that such a scheme would be called upon to do more than bridge the income gap for short periods of frictional unemployment.

Such optimism was short-lived. As the unemployment figures rose, many exhausted the limited period covered by insurance and had to be provided with other forms of 'benefit' from central government funds. The burden on the public purse grew. The National Economy Act 1931 reduced the benefits and soon after enforced a rigorous 'means test'. To understand the bitterness of the social controversy that followed this measure it is necessary to realise that the hated Poor Laws were still in the living memory of many, when no distinction had been made between those unable or unwilling to work and those thrown out 'of a job for economic reasons for which they could not be held responsible.

At the height of the depression in the thirties the official rate of unemployment was in most industrialised countries well over 20% of the labour force. Unemployment was partly frictional, of course, but particularly in areas where one heavy industry dominated the labour market, the rate was not only much higher – two-thirds permanently unemployed in Jarrow, famed for its hunger marches to the capital, 50 or 60% in coal-mining communities in South Wales, for example – but it also included a very high proportion of men unemployed for many years, some of them since the general strike in 1926. Unemployed miners over 45 years of age were resigned to never finding work again during their life-time.

In Great Britain physical deprivation in food and clothing were the rule, not the exception. A family of father, mother and three children, for example, received unemployment benefits to the amount of 29s 3d. The cost of feeding such a family was then calculated to be 20s 8d, and average rents amounted to 5s; this left 3s 7d for lighting, fuel, clothing and cleaning, a sum not sufficient to cover even this barest minimum of existence. Then as now it was the families with many children who suffered most. Husband and wife without children received 6s less benefit, but needed less for food and were left with 9s 1d, after rent, for other necessities of life. At the other extreme, a family with six children was on the same calculation left with a weekly *deficit* of 1s 11d. In one Welsh community, Pontypridd, which had in the early 1930s an unemployment rate of over 58%, routine medical school inspection identified malnutrition in 21% of the children (Save the Children International Union, 1933).

The situation was even worse in some other countries. In Poland, for example, with a lower national standard of living than that in Great Britain, the average daily caloric intake in a family with an employed breadwinner was 2,705; if he was unemployed, 1,951 calories. An enquiry among more than 15,000 school-children showed that 25% had had no breakfast at all, 5% had dry bread, another 50% tea without milk and dry bread. Another Polish study of unemployed families discovered that for each 100 girls investigated there were 88 pairs of shoes, for each 100 boys 95 pairs of boots. Fifty-four per cent of the children of Polish miners were absent from school owing to lack of clothes; among the weavers this percentage was 35 (Save the Children International Union, 1933). For Hungary, Garraty reports (1978, pp. 175–6) that according to trade union estimates those on relief – 18% of the population of Budapest – received about half the money required for a minimum standard of living.

In Austria, too, physical deprivation was amply documented. A medical investigation showed that 57% of children of the Viennese unemployed were under normal weight; in the Marienthal area this percentage was 76. The impossibility of proper budgeting under the conditions of insufficient allowances was demonstrated by a comparison of the lunches children brought to school on the day before the fortnightly allowance was paid and the day after: on the former 50% brought nothing to eat; on the latter this was reduced to 5%. When parents in Marienthal were asked whether unemployment had created any new problems in their relationships with their children, the only one they mentioned was how to keep growing boys from playing football, and thus entirely ruining their boots and clothes.

It must be noted, however, that there is some evidence contradicting the negative impact of long-term unemployment on health and nutrition. For Austria Stiefel (1979) concludes that the findings from special studies and official reports – the former showing negative impact, the latter not – cannot be reconciled, even though he inclines to the opinion that health was not seriously affected. Bakke (1933), who summarises official reports as well as his own observation in Greenwich, England, in 1931 concurs: 'The available information would indicate that the unusual amount of unemployment to which Great Britain has been subject during the last ten years has not to any appreciable degree injuriously affected the health of the schoolchildren' (p. 58). Health and nutrition of the adult unemployed were less often subjected to systematic study. Here and there some reports suggest that their health improved if unemployment occurred for people otherwise in unhealthy occupations. So the authors of the Marienthal study report:

> Work in a spinning or weaving mill . . . affects the respiratory tracts and the ear-splitting noise of the machines frays the nerves. People working in such factories are . . . exposed to the threat of tuberculosis; the doctor

stated that in the old days 90% . . . had been potential cases, but the situation had improved, people had become more healthy. The absence of factory work affecting the lungs and of heavy physical labour, coupled with a greater amount of time spent outdoors, has had a beneficial effect.

Actually, however, it is not too difficult to reconcile such contrasting evidence, as comparisons between the state of health at the beginning of the depression and a few years later indicate. Nutritional deficits take time before they undermine health. From the U.S.A. it is reported, for example, that by December 1930 milk consumption in New York City had dropped by a million quarts (Garraty, 1978, p. 175). Nonetheless, in 1932 the Surgeon General of the U.S.A. sounded an optimistic note about the health of the population: the mortality rate, which was 12 per 1,000 in 1929, had dropped to 10.6 by 1932 (Garraty, p.174). His report for the fiscal year 1935 (reviewed in Sydenstone, 1936), however, tells a different story. A series of studies on health among low-paid urban labour during the depression reported that the illness rate per person in families with unemployed workers was 48% above that in families with a full-time worker. There is also some indication in the report that mortality among the unemployed was higher than among the employed (p. 208). It must be noted, however, that these data do not demonstrate that unemployment caused illness and death; it is possible that those in poor health in the lowest paid occupations were more frequently made unemployed. There is indeed much evidence for the U.S.A., the U.K. and other countries that health and mortality are still closely related to occupational status.

There are, however, additional explanations for the discrepancy between general reports on the state of health of a nation and the findings of small, localised studies of the health of the unemployed. Some official inquiries reported national or regional averages, covering employed and unemployed together; any improvement in the former may well have disguised the situation of the latter. So, for example, a special commission charged by the Ministry of Health to investigate these matters in South Wales could note for the entire area in 1929 that the diet greatly lacked in fresh meat, fresh milk and fresh vegetables, but that its observations 'did not disclose any widespread manifestation of impaired health which could be attributed to insufficiency of nourishment' (quoted in Bakke, 1933, p. 52). It remains unclear

19

whether such impairment, where it was found, was randomly distributed or concentrated among the children of the long-term unemployed. Most of the small-scale inquiries concentrated on the worst-hit areas, often without the safeguard of a comparison group.

On the other hand there were some factors that mitigated the worst effects. Private charity and public help through, for example, school meals, may have improved nutrition beyond the purchasing power of the allowance. Furthermore, food prices fell drastically during the depression (in contrast to the present situation) so that the minimal budgets, established at an earlier moment in time, may gradually have lost to some degree their 'minimal' character.

Those who maintained that the effects of unemployment on health were small find support from Engels' law stating that the proportion of income spent on food rises in inverse relation to the size of income; accordingly, the unemployed may have foregone other necessities of life, such as fuel, clothing and rent, to a greater extent than the standardised budget assumed and spent more on food. Although this law is valid as a good macro-economic prediction of broad consumption trends in relation to income distribution, it assumes like so much macro-economic thought perfect rationality in consumption behaviour. Of course it would be perfectly rational if those with very low incomes spent what they had on a carefully calculated optimal diet. But in the micro-world of family budgeting rationality does not dominate, not with the rich and certainly not with the poor. To assume that all expenditure on small luxuries is cut out when unemployment hits amounts to a complete misunderstanding of human needs once utter starvation is out of the question. In Marienthal, for example, women who could not afford to buy milk for their children found little trinkets offered by a travelling salesman irresistible. Those who had allotments did not concentrate on vegetables only, but delighted in growing flowers: 'one can't just live on food, one needs also something for the soul', as one of them explained.

The idea that the hierarchy of human needs, established by Maslow (1958/70) and now often used in planning to ameliorate the poverty in the third world – beginning with the need for food and shelter and culminating in the need for self-actualisation – corresponds to a temporal sequence of what the underprivileged want from life, is psychologically mistaken and politically ultimately reactionary, according full human stature to only a small élite. The fact that many unemployed in the thirties lived a marginal existence did not prevent them from suffering through unfulfilled 'higher' needs, not even those who rationally restricted their food consumption to the cheapest available items and severely curtailed other expenditure.

In any case, however the evidence for the impact of unemployment on physical health is interpreted, there is no controversy over the fact that the unemployed experienced their condition as restrictive poverty and not just as the loss of regular occupation. The weight of the economic factor in influencing the overall psychological response to unemployment was demonstrated in Marienthal. There four types were distinguished: those unemployed whose morale was unbroken, the resigned, those in despair and the apathetic. The assessment of each family in these terms was based on multiple sources: home and household management observed by the investigators, money budgets, menus, time budgets, interviews and unobtrusive observations by participant observers. These four types showed a strong correlation with the amount of benefit or emergency assistance available per consumption unit in a family. If the monetary relief of those with unbroken morale is set at 100, that of the resigned was 88, of those in despair 74, and of the apathetic 56. Since it was in the nature of the Austrian system of support for the unemployed that its amount decreased over time though the hardship increased through the wear and tear on family belongings that could not be replaced – a feature still characteristic of some modern systems – one would predict from these figures a gradual deterioration of the psychological mood of the people in Marienthal.

Yet there is some evidence to show that the first effect of mass unemployment – the factory in this one-factory village had closed down in 1929, more than two years before the investigation was conducted – was even more extreme. People reacted with shock to the onset of unemployment. Women panicked about household management. Some got into debt, even though they learned to manage on reduced resources later on. Voluntary organisations and clubs closed their doors, though some opened them again a year later. One concludes that the process of adaptation to long-term unemployment has several stages: an immediate shock-reaction is followed by a slight recovery when people learn to manage somehow, but this adaptation is threatened as economic hardship increases. At least this was the case in Marienthal, where these matters were studied in considerable detail. There is, however, some support for the similar shape of this process from other studies in other countries.

An analysis of 57 autobiographies of unemployed workers in Warsaw shows six stages in their reaction to unemployment. The initial response is fear and distress; this is followed by numbness and apathy, gradually replaced by some adaptation and efforts to obtain employment. As the futility of such efforts becomes obvious, hope weakens. This is followed by complete loss of hope which gradually changes either to apathy or sober acquiescence (Zawadski and Lazarsfeld, 1935). A similar process is described for the unemployed in Italy (Gatti, 1937): surprise at becoming unemployed and fear are followed by some hope and efforts to get work; when such efforts fail anxiety increases and in the end apathy results.

The consequences of unemployment that have so far been described are intricately interwoven with the consequences of poverty. There are others, however, where the connection with poverty is less strong or, at least, less obvious.

Foremost among these other consequences is the enforced destruction of a habitual time structure for the waking day with the sudden onset of unemployment. In modern industrialised societies the experience of time is shaped by public institutions. Even before people begin to earn their living in employment the school system structures the day of a child; family and school co-operate – albeit with varying success – to impress on the young the value of punctuality and the need to fill the day with planned activities. Virtually all employment involves a fixed time schedule, often rigidly fixed by the requirement to clock in at the beginning and clock out at the end of the working day. Not only manual workers but everybody living in an industrialised society is used to firm time structures – and to complaining about them. But when this structure is removed as it is in unemployment its absence presents a major psychological burden. Days stretch long when there is nothing that has to be done; boredom and waste of time become the rule, particularly once the first shock has been overcome and the search for employment has been given up as futile.

In Marienthal the unemployed men lost their sense of time. Even though their time budgets were empty – filling, for example, the hours between getting up and the midday meal with an activity that could not have lasted more than 10 minutes – the women complained that their menfolk were unpunctual for meals. Time and time keeping had lost meaning. Since there was then still a strict division of labour for household tasks, unemployed women were less affected by this absence of time structure: they still had things that needed to be done and gave structure to their day. For the unemployed men the waking day was on the average reduced to $13\frac{1}{2}$ hours; sleeping kept them warm, saved their clothes and made them forget their worries. Of the 100 morning and 100 afternoon time periods reported about 80 of each were idled away either at home or on the street corner or in the working men's club. Even the weekend lost much of its structuring meaning and was replaced by the day on which allowances were paid once a fortnight.

Bakke, too, reports that in Greenwich the unemployed, particularly the unskilled, spent a good deal of their time on the streets, watching others and waiting for something to happen. He noted that there was little conversation during such idling. Cinema attendance where cheap afternoon tickets were available did not decrease. Killing 3 hours of time in a warm place with pleasant images for the price of 6d appeared to those who could afford it money well spent.

Now there is, of course, no external obstacle that prevents the unemployed from establishing their own time structure for engaging in hobbies and other types of meaningful work outside the contractual arrangements of employment. Indeed, in Marienthal some functionaries of political parties managed to do so. But these were rare exceptions, and for the vast majority of unemployed the destruction of their habitual time structure is experienced as a heavy psychological burden. To blame the unemployed for their inability to use their time in a more satisfactory way is pointless; it would amount to asking that they single-handedly overthrow the compelling social norms under which we all live and which provide a supportive frame within which individuals shape their individual lives. There are at all times only a few who can manage without it. Even with all their material and educational advantages some academics, freed for a year from their regular time structure, flounder and feel lost. To expect that the unemployed, the vast majority of whom are deprived of such privileges, could do better is unrealistic.

The time experience of the unemployed, often matched by the time experience of the retired even when they do not suffer economic hardship, should therefore not be regarded as leisure. Leisure hours are a complement to working hours, not a substitute for them. Indeed, part of their appeal consists of their relative scarcity. In all industrialised societies labour movements have striven to make them somewhat less scarce, while never abandoning their demand for full employment.

In addition to the destruction of a culturally imposed time structure, and in relation to it, the unemployed during the great depression suffered from a sense of purposelessness. The phrases repeated in virtually all studies are: being on the scrap-heap, useless, not needed by anybody. This was, of course, a perfectly realistic appraisal of the then existing economic situation, not a figment of their imaginations nor the result of their depressed standards of living. Industrialised societies, then as now, have often been described as emphasising individualism as a dominant value, but while this may be relatively correct if they are compared with societies organised on a tribal basis, it is at best a half-truth. The other half is indicated by the experience of the unemployed. An ever-increasing division of labour does not diminish but rather intensifies the essentially social needs and purposes of the human species. Just as leisure and employment are complementary and cannot be replaced by each other, so individualism needs to be embedded in a social context to be valued at all. Outside the nuclear family it is employment that provides for most people this social context and demonstrates in daily experience that 'no man is an island, entire of itself', that the purposes of a collectivity transcend the purposes of an individual. Deprived of this daily demonstration, the unemployed suffer from lack of purpose, exclusion from the larger society and relative social isolation.

There were, of course, individual differences with regard to this as well as local differences. The sense of isolation where almost the entire community is unemployed and all the neighbours are in the same boat may be less sharp than where an unemployed person lives among those who are employed, as was the case in Greenwich, where one of the men said: 'you are not human [when unemployed]. You're out of place. You're so different from all the rest of the people around that you think something is wrong with you. I don't care what your job is, you feel a lot more important when you come home at night than if you had been tramping around the streets all day' (Bakke, 1933, p. 63). In Marienthal the absence of a required pursuit of collective purposes interfered even with the continuation of private purposes for which time had been found during previous employment. So while the local library had abolished former borrowing charges, the number of readers dropped with the length of unemployment; even the few who continued to use the library borrowed fewer books than before. Subscription to daily papers, though offered to the unemployed at a much reduced price, dropped by 60%; political organisations and clubs lost between one-third and two-thirds of their membership.

In the absence of the regular contact with a collectivity and its purposes, the social experience of the unemployed shrank, particularly in cases where an unemployed person lived among people who were still employed. It was frequently reported that such relatively isolated unemployed experienced shame and self-doubt that led them to withdrawal from former social relations. But whether or not self-confidence was undermined, the scope for shared social experience was reduced. In employment, even a shy and withdrawn person cannot help but enlarge his knowledge of the social world as he observes the similarities or differences, compared with his own, of the habits, opinions and life experience of others around him. He may not like the social contacts that employment enforces, but they are an inescapable source for enlarging his social horizon. During unemployment such impoverishment of social experience follows necessarily from the change in the structure of daily life. Few, if any, of the unemployed could indicate this beyond saying that they missed their previous contacts with their colleagues.

Indirect support for the experience of deprivation involved in an enforced narrowing of social contacts comes from the growing number of articulate women who describe it as the major psychological burden in bringing up small children, however great their love for them. Equally, housewives whose children have grown up often suffer most from their lack of social contacts with the world outside their four walls. Neither group of women is, of course, short of work. It appears that for women as well as for men, home life is a complement to wider social contacts, not a generally acceptable substitute for them, parallel to the relation between employment and leisure. One reason why family relations cannot replace the need for wider contacts such as employment provides lies in the different nature of these two types of human relations: family relations are as a rule much more emotionally charged than relations with others in employment. For better or worse, family relations enrich or impoverish emotional life; the emotionally calmer climate of relations with colleagues provides more information, more opportunity for judgement and rational appraisal of other human beings with their various foibles, opinions and ways of life.

Related to some of these psychological consequences is the often noted loss of status and identity as a result of unemployment. This is not surprising given the structure of modern industrial societies in which status and prestige are defined in the public eye by the nature of the job that a person holds. While status is essentially a social phenomenon anchored in the value system of a society, identity is a more personal notion that refers as a rule to people's images of themselves. The two notions are thus conceptually distinct; in the experience of people, however, social status and personal identity are closely intertwined. Because of widespread consensus in public life about the social status assigned to varying jobs, people tend to adopt this assignation as one clear element in defining themselves to themselves and are reluctant to dispense with this support for their personal identity. In Marienthal, the unemployed were asked on their time budget sheets to state their occupation, with the idea of separating the skilled from the unskilled. It was a technical mistake not to ask for the occupation in last employment, but a mistake that bore fruit. About a quarter of the unemployed stated their trade; they were either the very young who had finished an apprenticeship, had no job but had not given up hope, or men over 50 for whom the identification with their trade was of long standing. Those between 21 and 50 tended to identify themselves as 'unemployed'. This adaptation in the middle years to unemployment as a status and self-definition, and thereby to being outsiders to normal life, is evidence for the social disintegration that went in that community with long-term unemployment.

Most of the evidence for the impact of unemployment in the thirties concerns manual workers. Office employees, supervisors, managers, executive and other professional occupations were then, of course, also affected by unemployment. In the absence of evidence one can only speculate that the loss of status from a higher place in the occupational hierarchy may have been felt as even harder to take. There were, however, compensating factors for those in the so-called higher occupations. Not only is it plausible to assume that their material deprivation was on the whole less severe; to the extent that their activities in employment involved their special training, knowledge and expertise – assets largely independent from materials and capital equipment – they could, at least in principle, continue while unemployed some of the activities they had had during employment. No miner could operate his trade when the mine closed; no textile worker could continue without his loom. It stands to reason that the nature of the activity in which an unemployed person was previously engaged must have a bearing on the way in which he experiences its cessation. I shall return to this point later on. Here it should only be emphasised that the available evidence for manual workers points to a sharp break between activities before and after unemployment, and often to the absence of all regular activities.

Given the extent of unemployment during the depression not only its economic consequences but also its psychological effects stopped being only a matter for private lives and became a social issue of large proportions. At the time public debates in several countries were split into two camps: some, convinced that the situation was intolerable for the unemployed, predicted that it would lead to social revolution; others, aware of the fact that security of employment had never existed in modern times, certainly not since the beginning of the industrial revolution, thought that the unemployed lacked both the individual and the organisational strength to spearhead a revolution and limited their concern to consequences for the national economy, though not always without compassion for the plight of those most directly affected.

In this respect studies in several countries emerged with an unambiguous answer: mass unemployment led to resignation in personal lives and in social matters, not to revolution. Of course there was some agitation in several countries aiming to turn the plight of the unemployed into revolutionary fervour, but without success. Bakke reports for Greenwich that the political attitudes of the unemployed were indistinguishable from those of the employed. Among the unemployed studied in Poland there was some tendency to be more critical of their government, but not to become revolutionaries. A historical analysis of the situation in the U.S.A. (Hallgren, 1933) branded the idea that hunger leads to revolt as a myth. Neither was there any sign of revolutionary fervour in Marienthal. A comparison of voting behaviour in 1929 (the year before the factory there closed down) and in 1932 showed virtually identical party loyalties: in both years 80% voted for the social democratic party. The unhappy political events in Austria nonetheless demonstrated that mass unemployment can have disastrous political consequences. When Hitler invaded Austria in 1938 large portions of the population welcomed him, including the population of Marienthal. Hitler came with soup-kitchens and the promise of work, a promise redeemed within the first year of the occupation in the interest of building up his war machine, the road system and bridges that his plans required. Almost fifty years later the people of Marienthal made it quite clear that they would have supported anybody who gave them employment; ideological commitments had little relevance to their life situation.

To round off this retrospect to the meaning of unemployment during the depression years of the thirties it is appropriate to consider some of the policies that were then suggested or implemented to deal with the situation. This is not the place to attempt a systematic analysis of the economic and political thought at that time on which the various policies were based. Others have dealt with such matters in depth much more adequately than I could hope to do; Garraty (1978) has analysed unemployment policies during the depression, and before, on an international basis; there exists an enormous literature on the policies of Roosevelt's New Deal in the U.S.A.; Stiefel (1979) has recently written a book on the history of unemployment in Austria between 1918 and 1938 in which the struggle about policies is fully documented. What is in place here is a brief examination of the social-psychological impact of various types of policy on the life situation of the unemployed.

This situation, as I have tried to show, was dominated by two related major factors: an inadequate standard of living and the psychological impact of being without a job. It stands to reason that only the creation of jobs could change both at one stroke. But this appeared to government and industry to be beyond their economic power; even the New Deal managed to create jobs only for a relatively small minority of unemployed people. In 1933 the estimates of unemployment figures in the U.S.A. varied between 13 and 16 million; in 1933/4 the Civil Works administration catered for 4 million. In Britain comparable efforts never provided for more than 59,000. Only in Sweden and in Hitler's Germany were there massive public works programmes (Garraty, 1978, p. 206). Recognising that the optimal solution was elsewhere beyond reach, the political struggle was about appropriate partial measures, largely concerned with the amount of unemployment allowance, but in recognition of the psychological impact of being for many years without a job, also with work-creation and training, particularly for the young.

Adequate allowances inevitably increase the economic burden on the tax-payer, but the arguments against were even then, as now, often conducted in terms of their assumed deleterious psychological impact on the motivation to work, as if the individual's will to work could have created jobs where economic policies failed. It was true then, as it is now, that welfare policies were abused by a few. But the suspicion that this would be the case was then much greater than warranted by established facts. In the social disintegration that resulted from long-term unemployment in Marienthal this suspicion was expressed in the tripling of the number of anonymous denunciations to the authorities that somebody had found casual employment in neighbouring villages while drawing unemployment relief. On investigation it was discovered that three-quarters of such denunciations were unfounded. By comparison the proportion of unfounded accusations from the Marienthal population in the year before the factory closed down was one-third. Even if in Marienthal it was the suspicion of abuse rather than the number of abuses that had increased by 1932, it is not unlikely that in the following six years of unemployment in which material deprivation became worse, abuses too would have become more frequent, as long as there was somewhere some opportunity for casual earnings.

There was – unfortunately from the point of view of the unemployed – no opportunity then to test the broader suspicion that a more adequate allowance would destroy the will to work. With the lengthening of the depression allowances were reduced or even eliminated, not increased.

Then, as now, there was widespread agreement that the impact of unemployment on children and young people might be psychologically most damaging and required, therefore, special measures. Studies in

29

Employment and unemployment

Germany before Hitler came into power had demonstrated that the school performance of children deteriorated with the onset of parental unemployment, particularly among those whose previous performance had been good, as indicated by their marks; a renewed deterioration occurred when parental unemployment had lasted three or more years (Eisenberg and Lazarsfeld, 1938, p. 381). This effect was attributed to inadequate nutrition, even though its very fast onset suggests that the inpact of unemployment on the family atmosphere may have been a contributing cause. Whatever the reason, in Germany and elsewhere school meals, financed from public and private sources, were provided to alleviate the nutritional deficit; in many countries private collections of second-hand clothing were organised and distributed to the children of the unemployed, as well as to their parents. However helpful such compassionate gestures were in alleviating the worst economic misery, they bore the stigma of poor relief and must have intensified in the unemployed their sense of being outside the normal order, unable to share in the collective purposes and rewards of the wider community.

For young people, many of whom had never held a job after leaving school, a variety of schemes were introduced in several countries. Voluntary organisations, some political parties and some trade unions established youth clubs to keep the young men and women off the streets. As a minimum such clubs provided warmth and company; sometimes also some food, sports facilities and occasional lectures or films. Once again: undoubtedly helpful, but neither offering economic independence nor pointing the way to a future in which such independence could be achieved.

There was at the time much concern that these young people who had never acquired the habit of holding a job would be not able or not willing to acquire one when the depression receded but would prefer to continue their unstructured idle lives. This is why some organised activities for the young were widely advocated and sometimes realised so as to counteract the psychological impact of unemployment. The Austrian government, for example, established a public works programme for those young people who had never been in employment. Camps were established in which food, working clothes and lodgings were provided, but no wages paid, for a six-hour working day. It soon emerged that this scheme, suspected by many to amount to conscription for paramilitary purposes, was economically not viable. It would have been cheaper to have these useful public works performed by people paid the full rate for the job, but who lived their ordinary family life. There is no evidence to show whether it had psychologically constructive consequences. One may well doubt it since it denied the young the independence and freedom of movement they enjoy after a working day in normal employment.

There is, however, some evidence about the functioning of a voluntary scheme in South Wales designed to alleviate both the economic and the psychological burden of long-term unemployment (Jahoda, 1938). In 1935 a small group of Quakers, deeply concerned with the futility of life among former miners who had been unemployed for years, started a Subsistence Production Society. The leading idea was to organise and finance a co-operative enterprise, manned by the unemployed to produce goods and services for their own subsistence, but not for sale on the open market. The 400 voluntary members of the scheme received no wages; they were entitled to draw their normal unemployment allowance. In addition they could buy the results of their own productive labour for the cost of the raw materials to which 20% was added for overheads. On the average this increased the purchasing power of their unemployment allowance by about one-third. The amount of economic benefit varied with the size of a man's family: a man with four children could buy more milk or bread and could get more shoes repaired than one with no children, but everybody was expected to work a thirty-hour week. This amounted to an effort to implement the great ideals of socialism that everybody should contribute according to his ability and receive according to his need and that production should be for use, not for profit.

Given that the financial benefit to the members was less than in ordinary employment and independent of their qualifications, efforts and skills, the question arises whether this scheme could eliminate at least the psychological consequences of unemployment. To an extent it succeeded with some, but it failed with more. Absenteeism was high, 24% in an average week, particularly among those under 45 years of age. It was in all respects the older men who had resigned themselves to spending the rest of their lives on the dole before the scheme started who tended to benefit psychologically from it. They, more than the younger ones, welcomed the time structure for the day that the scheme provided. All members were enabled to widen their social experiences

31

through their daily close contact with the Quaker organisers who were always ready to discuss their ideas about new forms of industrial relations and there was regular contact with other members of the teams; many enjoyed the open-air activities that were in such sharp contrast to labouring underground, or the various new skills they could acquire, such as weaving or bricklaying. But two of the psychological burdens that unemployment imposes – the undermining of status and identity and the exclusion from the purposes of the larger society – were perhaps even intensified by membership in the scheme. The resulting conflict of ideas in the minds of the unemployed was largely responsible for a considerable number of abuses: not only bad time-keeping, but much loafing, selling of goods to outsiders, some pilfering and waste of raw materials made the cost of the scheme, in spite of some governmental financial support, prohibitive. Notwithstanding their virtually unanimously professed socialist convictions these unemployed miners were steeped in the traditions of capitalism that had for generations split them from the bosses and induced them to fight against often brutal exploitation. These long-established habits of thought made them wonder whether they had involved themselves through membership in the Quaker scheme in a subtler form of exploitation and led them to distrust the Quaker organisers, though their gentle manner was in sharp contrast to the treatment they had previously experienced from the mine-owners.

The scheme was threatened with closure for lack of funds when the outbreak of the Second World War brought it to an end and employment in the mines or in the forces was once again available.

That this impressive social experiment must ultimately be judged to have failed does not imply that efforts to create a new climate for industrial relations on a limited experimental basis must always fail. Producer co-operatives, such as Mondragon, the co-operative in the Basque country, prove the contrary. There were several reasons that made the Subsistence Production Society in the end into just another temporary charity for the unemployed. Perhaps the most important was that men who had suffered for years the psychological damage of unemployment had lost the strength and conviction required to support wholeheartedly a new creative social experiment.

4

Employment and unemployment in the nineteen-eighties

> We entered Marienthal as scientists; we leave it with only one desire:
> that the tragic opportunity for such an inquiry may not recur in our time.

Half a century after these words were written the hope that they embodied, and that for twenty years after the last war seemed fulfilled, has been bitterly disappointed. While the national rates of unemployment are nowhere as high as they were then, the experience of people is always more influenced by their immediate environment than by national averages; and in their immediate neighbourhoods many experience a dimension of unemployment comparable to that in Marienthal while others in more fortunate localities experience unemployment much as elsewhere in the thirties against the background of jobs for the majority within their immediate surroundings. The difference in numbers and rates can, therefore, not be expected to produce qualitative changes in the experience of being unemployed.

Much else has, however, so radically changed that from a social-psychological perspective it is reasonable to enquire whether the experiences of the thirties are being replicated now. What are these changes?

First among them are the changes in material circumstances. Notwithstanding the enormous social and economic problems that beset the modern world the standard of living in industrialised countries, including that of their unemployed, has dramatically improved in the last half-century. This is most tellingly summarised by life expectancy figures. In Great Britain a boy born in 1931 could expect to live 58 years, a girl 62 years; now these figures are over 70 years, with about the same difference between the sexes, even though the social class differences in this respect have not been eliminated.

This improvement is in part the result of national health services, available to all in Great Britain and in many other countries, thus excluding the catastrophic impact of illness on the unemployed in the previous period; in part it is due to widely improved nutritional standards as a result of the general rise in the standard of living. But it would be wrong to conclude that unemployment now has been completely uncoupled from poverty, though it is less strongly and less frequently linked to it.

In the thirties unemployment insurance was not yet universal. The U.S.A. introduced a national unemployment insurance law only in 1935. Now such schemes are almost universal, even though as a rule limited to the first six months or one year of the unemployment; after that period public assistance at reduced amounts is normally available. The insurance benefit is earnings linked (recently abolished in Great Britain) and in many countries automatically inflation indexed (recently curtailed in Britain). Redundancy payments according to seniority are often available and help to ease the transition to a lower standard of living. It should be noted, parenthetically, that the dependence on years of employment of the amount of redundancy payment is one of the many factors that interfere with the often desirable mobility of labour.

A system of earnings-related benefits favours the higher paid skilled workers when unemployment hits; unskilled workers, particularly casual and disabled workers, do even now experience poverty, though perhaps not of the extreme type that prevailed in the thirties. In a recent collection of life histories of English unemployed people it is stated that the less skilled could not be adequately maintained on supplementary benefits. 'Families slipped into debt, with a routine of court orders and growing dilapidation of furnishings. For a proportion of the families there was real hardship, with a shortage of money for food, clothing and electricity' (Marsden and Duff, 1975, p. 238). These life histories were collected in 1972; it may well be worse to-day. In any case, even if from an observer's point of view poverty as a result of unemployment is now less devastating than it was in the thirties, from the point of view of those who experience a reduction by half of their income that was in the majority of cases already low compared with average incomes, the relative deprivation is severe indeed, even when absolute deprivation is avoided.

Another significant change is the addition of two years to compulsory education. It is true that some youngsters do not profit much from this extension but the great majority do in knowledge, maturity and aspirations. The growth of further and tertiary education enhances these qualities in a proportion of the young. There can be no question that the educational level of the entire population has risen, even if some rightly say not enough, and others too much. The fact remains that aspirations rise with the level of education.

Young people who are now between 16 and 30 years of age grew up in a period of relatively full employment which may have further increased their expectations of finding employment as their parents did. How pervasive the confidence in relatively full employment was during the two extraordinary decades that followed the Second World War is illustrated by a quotation from an excellent book on the social psychology of industry that appeared first in 1954. Discussing methods of maintaining industrial discipline the author says that the fear of unemployment is for that purpose 'no longer practicable . . . because it seems certain that any future government of this country will be compelled, so far as possible, to maintain full employment' (J. A. C. Brown, 1954, p. 18). At the same time a study of an English steel-works found little evidence of hostility to the introduction of new technology even if it led to redundancies (Banks, 1960), because it was so easy to find other jobs.

No wonder, then, that the expectation of finding employment was widespread in that generation. When it nevertheless became impossible for many to find or to hold a job two somewhat opposite effects can be assumed. On the one hand, unemployment may be psychologically more difficult to take if it frustrates high hopes; on the other hand the better educated may have developed inner resources and wider horizons that may help them to mitigate some of its psychological consequences. There is as yet little empirical material available to test these speculations.

Not only has formal education increased but also the entire population's knowledge of the world, particularly of how other people live. During the great depression television had not yet been heard of; now it is virtually universal. Social scientists have investigated the impact of television in a variety of ways, understandably largely focussing on the great amount of violence on the screen. But the visual display of comfortable middle class standards of living, inadvertently presented as the way to live through studio furniture or clothes of announcers and as the background to many serious and many entertaining programmes, together with visual advertising of consumer goods – so much more powerful than the written or spoken word – must have affected the material aspirations of many and become the standard against which they experience their own relative deprivation.

The heightened level of aspiration is one aspect of a fundamental change in the ethos of modern industrial societies, a change so often convincingly asserted that one tends to forget how difficult it is to obtain solid evidence for it. Among the many aspects of this change – consumerism, progressive secularisation, change of sexual mores, the demise of the deferential society, widespread alienation – the most relevant in the present context is the assertion that the work ethic as a unifying social norm is on the way out. Pampered by the welfare state – so the argument goes – people do not want to work. Many social scientists maintain, with or without evidence, that while in the past under the influence of Protestantism work was regarded as morally good, this notion is disappearing from the modern world; even if it still exists in some people in some occupations, its previous power to provide a social consensus has disappeared. In *The Social Limits to Growth* Hirsch (1977) argued forcefully that the twentieth century had borrowed the morality of the nineteenth but could no longer maintain it; it was now breaking down in favour of everyone competing with everyone else for top-level consumption of goods and positions, a palpably impossible aim that may lead to anarchy. Others (e.g. Kelvin, 1980) also assert that the work ethic has disappeared, that with an assumed inevitability of further growth in unemployment rates it will become 'respectable' to be unemployed, the stigma of poor relief will finally be removed from public support and that leisure activities will have to be developed or invented that can replace the role of employment in peoples' lives.

While recognising the force of such analyses of the shift in basic values, it is doubtful that all available evidence has been taken into account or that the assumptions about the past are correct. An example of the former is the evidence from many surveys that people want to work, even if it were not an economic necessity. Among the hard-core unemployed in the U.S.A. this proportion is reported as 84% (Kanter,

1978); as 74% in West Germany (Heinemann, 1978). Furthermore, there is a growing incidence of organised industrial action in favour of employment, from the take-over of factories under workers' control to strikes against redundancies or even violent action as in the case of the redundancies in the French steel industry. None of these results and actions supports the idea that people have lost their willingness to work.

Even the generality of the work ethic in the past is, perhaps, overemphasised so as to sharpen the contrast with the present. Can one really assume that those employed in the factories and mines under the brutal conditions of early-nineteenth-century capitalism shared the moral conviction about the virtue of being employed? Some doubts in this direction seem justified. On the other hand, however, under very different cultural conditions, as for example in Japan, an apparently universal work ethic seems to permeate this highly developed modern capitalist society, where employers find it difficult to keep their labour force away during legitimate holidays.

Notwithstanding such doubts about a change in the work ethic the notion of 'voluntary unemployment' plays a considerable role in the current public debate. Voluntary unemployment is a concept in theoretical economics that is based on considerations stemming from the simultaneous existence of unemployment and vacancies in the national economy and on the fact that benefits now amount to a higher proportion of average wages than in the past. However justified its theoretical meaning, the implications of the term 'voluntary' are regrettable. For, in common parlance, 'voluntary' implies that individuals consciously and deliberately decide that they prefer being unemployed.

It has been calculated for Great Britain (Hawkins, 1979) (albeit before the recent deterioration in the amount of unemployment benefit) that about 10% of the registered unemployed would be as well off, or better, on claiming all possible benefits than they would be in employment. That not all in this position make such rational calculations is demonstrated by the fact that the value of unclaimed supplementary benefits amounts to a considerable sum, estimated at £90 million in 1977 (Showler and Sinfield, 1981, p.83). Against the theoretical maximum of 10%, a sample survey (D. J. Smith, 1981, p. 54) found that 'only 3% of white men and 5% of minority group men

37

were receiving more in benefits than they had previously earned'.

Even if one adds to those entitled to live better in unemployment than in employment (they are mostly heads of large families in the worst-paid occupations) the small number of drop-outs and scroungers who settle for a lower standard of living rather than take a job, it would be preposterous to assume that the vast number of the currently unemployed are voluntarily so. In any case, in human affairs 'voluntary' decisions have a scope severely restricted by compelling social norms and compelling individual past life experiences; what little remains is very important, but certainly not large enough to explain the current rise in unemployment as due to voluntary decisions. The difficulty of making a sharp distinction between voluntary and involuntary actions besets all psychological thought. There exist in modern industrialised societies types of jobs that many perform only under the compulsion of economic necessity. Should such activities be described as 'voluntary' or 'involuntary'?

So there remains a doubt about regarding the currently prevailing work ethic as fundamentally changed from that in the thirties; it is, therefore, not a reason to assume that the experience of unemployment is now different from what it was then. The change from absolute physical deprivation to relative deprivation for large numbers of the unemployed, on the other hand, is such a reason. So is the higher level of aspiration in a better educated and healthier population. This will undoubtedly influence the types of jobs people are ready and able to perform and the conditions of employment they are willing to accept, but not necessarily their readiness for employment *per se*. The very large number of women who have now entered the labour market, a probably irreversible change from the past, is further evidence for the growing wish for employment which is largely but not exclusively a matter of income. Furthermore, with a more articulate population social deference to those in privileged positions must have been significantly reduced, a change that may affect the psychological consequences of unemployment by making self-blame for being unemployed less frequent.

The impact of these changes is of course not restricted to the experience of unemployment; it is felt throughout modern life but particularly in employment, which is still the rule for the vast majority of the population. Since modern employment conditions are the experiental reference point with which the unemployed compare their current life situation, it stands to reason that the one cannot be discussed without the other.

It should be recalled that five aspects of the experience of unemployment in the thirties have been singled out: the experience of time, the reduction of social contacts, the lack of participation in collective purposes, the absence of an acceptable status and its consequences for personal identity, and the absence of regular activity. In all these aspects the unemployed felt psychologically deprived.

Employment as a social institution does not exist for the purpose of providing these categories of experience; its *raison d'être* is the provision of goods and services largely for profit. But as an unintended though inevitable consequence of its own purposes and organisation it enforces these categories of experience on all participants. While the unemployed are left to their own devices to find experiences within these categories if they can and suffer if they cannot, the employed take them for granted. What preoccupies them is not the category but the quality of the experience within it. When an unemployed man says 'I miss the people at work. Even the people I didn't like, I miss them' (Marsden and Duff, 1975, p. 177) he speaks about the absence of a category; when an employed man complains about his foreman, he objects to the quality of experience within the same category. Similarly the unemployed often experience boredom, that is the absence of time structure and regular activity; employed people comment on the quality of the imposed time structure and the content of their activities.

Conditions of employment have significantly improved in the industrialised world during the last half-century, in no small measure due to the activities of trade unions, particularly in the two decades of full employment. Wages are by and large more adequate, hours have been reduced and physical conditions are as a rule under public control and much better than they used to be. But the fact remains that the quality of employment experiences in some types of jobs and some organisations is as bad as in the thirties. Two, perhaps extreme, examples must suffice.

In 1957 the following exchange occurred in a U.S.A. Senate Investigating Committee between Robert Kennedy as counsel and an attorney representing a firm:

Mr Kennedy:	You say that the men can put the [enamel] equipment in the oven, then they can step back and eat their lunch during that period of time. How much time is there then before they have to do some more work?
Mr Conger:	From 2 to 5 minutes, depending on the piece.
Mr Kennedy:	So you feel they can step back from the oven, take off their masks and have their lunch in 2 to 5 minutes?
Mr Conger:	Mr Kennedy, they have been doing it for 36 years.

(Schlesinger, 1978, p. 179)

The second example comes from France. In 1969, a year after the *événements*, a Citroën plant decided to recuperate money they had paid to strikers in 1968 under the impact of these events, money that the strikers had regarded as their due. Management announced that the working day was to be prolonged by 45 minutes, half of it paid at normal rates, half to be the firm's recuperation of money paid during the strike (Linhart, 1976, pp. 75–6).

The point of quoting these examples is not to suggest that they are typical for modern industry – they are not; for all one knows they may even have been unique in their day. The point is to emphasise that before the Second World War similar conditions were frequent, have entered into the lore of manual labour, led to militant unionism, are still in the living memory of many and *to the extent* that such practices still exist make it doubtful whether the psychological burden of unemployment is indeed greater than that in such employment, though it is different in kind. But what is that extent?

It is impossible, of course, to give a precise answer to this question and therefore relatively easy to assert that alienation is virtually universal. Such assertions come not only from radical individuals but also from some observational studies. Ivan Illich is an example of the former, but not the only one. His iconoclastic voice has found an echo in a professor of business studies in the U.K. who has denounced employment as an institution from whose 'destructive embrace' people should be freed and suggested that 'instead of rejecting the new unemployed as parasitic we will need to romanticise them as an élite moving into the unknown' (Pym, 1975, p. 698). He does not say what else to put in the place of employment, but since he also deplores literacy's 'villainous role in our troubles' perhaps a return to more primitive forms of communal living is in his mind. Short of a nuclear

40

catastrophe the probability of such a transformation seems remote.

There also exist several studies based on the direct experience of investigators who have taken a job on the shopfloor to see for themselves what it is like. The emerging picture is horrifying: employment is degraded and degrading. In 1977 two studies appeared, one by a Hungarian (Haraszti, 1977) one by a Swede (Palm, 1977), reporting on a year's experience in industry. Even though the objective conditions were miles apart – almost intolerable in Hungary and reasonably comfortable in Sweden – their experiences were much alike: work on these shopfloors was physically exhausting and soul-destroying, whether done under a communist or a capitalist regime. A Frenchman (Linhart, 1976) who took a factory job, admittedly from political motives, describes much the same, as does a more recent of these impressionistic accounts by an American (Pfeffer, 1979). They all agree on the terrible time pressure to which production workers are subjected, particularly when on piecework or on conveyor-belt-type production; but even worse and more humiliating is the manner in which these manual workers are treated by those higher in the industrial hierarchy. All these authors feel that contempt and mistrust for the manual worker is built into the system. Workers are transferred to another job without explanation; are called into an office but kept waiting without being offered a chair, while the foreman continues with some paper work; are explicitly forbidden to whistle at work. To the workers, so these authors report, all this appears not just as bad behaviour and thoughtlessness but deliberately designed to make them feel a lesser breed than salaried personnel. Shopfloor workers, according to these reports, reciprocate with sharp resentment against those who do the 'easy' jobs in industry.

And yet, hidden in this contempt for those who do the 'easy' jobs, there is a sense of pride in manual work. Only one of the Swedish workers could put this into words. After hours of describing his deep frustration he suddenly discovered that he had omitted to mention his basic feelings about work and he insisted on adding:

> I want to work, I like work. I don't want to sit at home . . . I want to work in manufacturing industry, make things . . . to make the thing itself, to stand there in the centre, that is something special . . . I like to work with machines . . . all workers . . . want to do something useful, do a good job . . . But the management . . . they encourage the wrong things in the

worker ... why can't they understand, increased production, it could be a
lot if that respect was given to the worker ...   (Palm, 1977)

There is no reason to doubt the veracity of these observational
reports; but it is of course an ineluctable fact of life that intellectuals
seeking jobs in industry for a limited period are restricted to the most
unskilled jobs available. These are the jobs that carry in their
psychological consequences the brunt of the progressive division of
labour in industry that could, as Adam Smith recognised already in
1776, make a man 'as stupid and ignorant as it is possible for a human
creature to become' (Smith, 1776/1937).

Even though the working day is now very much shorter than it was in
the eighteenth century there are a number of modern studies that
support the direction of causality that Adam Smith suggested from the
nature of the job to the attributes of a person rather than the idea that
people in unskilled jobs on the lowest level of the industrial hierarchy
are not capable of doing anything else. Foremost among them is Arthur
Kornhauser's pioneering study (1965) on the mental health of car-
workers in Detroit. He distinguished several levels in the industrial
hierarchy and found on all his criteria of positive mental health that the
unskilled scored lowest. He enquired into the direction of causality and
could argue persuasively that it was the nature of the jobs that lowered
the human qualities of their occupants, not the other way round.

The same idea is expressed in the apt title of a study of the leisure
activities of skilled and unskilled workers: 'The Long Arm of the Job'
describes the passivity and impoverished nature of the leisure hours of
the unskilled (Meissner, 1971).

To the extent that these findings can be generalised for low-level
unskilled jobs they point to latent consequences of employment not
only on the individual but also on the social level. By virtue of such
employment there exists a stratum of society – its size is hard to
determine – of degraded, frustrated, unhappy, psychologically unhealthy people in employment whose personal morale is as low as their
productivity, who are unable to provide a constructive environment for
their families, whose lack of commitment in employment colours their
total life experience and, depending on the size of the group, the level
of civilisation of the society in which they live. This is increasingly
recognised by employers and job seekers. Many industrialised societies

have tried before unemployment became a major issue in the not too distant past to 'export' these negative consequences of employment by hiring guestworkers from less industrialised countries; others have used their own underprivileged minority groups in such employment, thereby – not surprisingly – increasing internal social tension.

That modern technology may eliminate one day the need for human beings performing most of the soul-destroying tasks under soul-destroying conditions is its brightest promise; its greatest danger is that it may replace unskilled labour by even higher unemployment rates as well as reducing the skill level for whatever jobs remain to be done.

Pfeffer, the author of the American impressionistic account, concludes from his interesting observations about degrading conditions in the plant in which he worked that only a Marxist revolution can humanise conditions of employment.

Even those who agree with his conclusion should ask themselves who will make that revolution: those who through economic necessity and 'false consciousness' do anything not to lose their jobs though they hate them and the dehumanising atmosphere that goes with them that has demoralised them? Waiting for that revolution is like waiting for Godot, and no substitute for changing conditions now by adopting deliberately the purpose of humanisation; and nobody knows what would happen if Godot ever came.

Since there can be little doubt that some types of jobs under some modern conditions are psychologically destructive, a controversy has arisen over the question of whether current indicators of social pathology are better explained by prevailing employment conditions or by rates of unemployment.

Harvey Brenner (1976) has related several of these indicators to unemployment rates with the introduction of a time lag. Brenner reasons that if unemployment as a stress-inducing condition were a causal factor in social pathology, its symptoms should not appear simultaneously but would need time to develop. Depending on the specific symptom, his assumed time lags vary from one to fifteen years. On aggregate the statistical associations which Brenner derives from a multivariate regression reveal, for example, that a single percentage increase in the unemployment rate in the U.S.A. if maintained over six years, could be associated with an increase in mortality affecting nearly 37,000 individuals. The relationship between economic instability and social pathology is complicated, however, as Brenner realises, and it would be wrong to point to unemployment as the sole variable. When he disaggregates his data, the overall correlation does not hold for all sub-groups and is even sometimes reversed. For example, although a study of the relationship between participation in manufacturing employment and admission to mental hospitals in New York State (Brenner, cited in Catalano and Dooley, 1977) found a negative correlation between first admission and such employment, the strength of this association varied within the population. For some groups (those with little formal education) the correlation was in fact reversed, lending some support to the debilitating impact of employment conditions on those with low skills.

That caution is always required when interpreting various macro-indicators is illustrated by studies relating the consumption of alcoholic beverage to the state of the economy. The historical context and cultural variations may be at the root of empirical associations which, therefore, must not be generalised to other times and other places. For example, Brenner found that over a *long* period alcohol intake in the U.S.A. is positively related to *per capita* income, while during relatively short recessions *per capita* alcohol consumption (and the form in which alcohol is consumed) is directly related to unemployment rates.

As for studies on the relations between crime and unemployment, included in Brenner's indicators of social pathology, the situation is highly complex for several reasons. Foremost among these are the notorious difficulties of crime statistics: many more crimes are committed than are known to the police; many more are known than lead to arrest; more come to the courts than are convicted. But whether the person involved was employed or unemployed is normally recorded in crime statistics only for this last, much reduced group.

The notion that unemployment leads to crime is, however, of long standing. Already in 1828, for example, the Lord Mayor of Breslau said in a report (quoted by Lüdtke, 1979): 'The presence here of so many unemployed, who are for the most part under the vigilant supervision of the police, but are so difficult to supervise . . . represents a dangerous threat'.

Newspaper reports of individual cases and editorial opinions in many countries support much the same views in the 1970s. It is indeed a reasonable assumption that those who have not got enough should be tempted to take it from those who have, but while this was demonstrated to be so in the nineteenth century during periods of high unemployment (Wacker, 1981, p. 252), when thefts and property crimes rose significantly, the relationship has diminished, if not disappeared, according to some studies in this century. In Austria, for example, there was between 1921 and 1928 a negative correlation between such crimes and the unemployment rate.

In some contrast in the U.S.A., between 1920 and 1931 thefts did increase with the unemployment rate, though there was a reduction in juvenile delinquency from 1929 onwards. In discussing these and other studies Wacker comes to the conclusion that the still prevalent idea that unemployment leads to crime is too simplistic – certainly when global crime rates are correlated with global unemployment rates.

There are a number of studies that have therefore rightly concentrated not on the correlation of overall rates but on the unemployment status of convicted offenders. An investigation of 560 juvenile delinquents in West Germany, for example (Heinemann, 1978), discovered that 27% of them were unemployed, a higher percentage than that of youth unemployment. By the same token, however, 73% of these youngsters committed crimes even though employed. Clearly unemployment alone is an insufficient explanation, otherwise the fast rise of criminality in the U.K. during the period of relatively full employment would defy understanding. Family background, living in a bad neighbourhood, lack of success in school and employment are contributing causes, as is the visible affluence of others, whether or not the offender is employed.

The theory behind Brenner's work has come under criticism, most explicitly by Eyer (1977*a*,*b*) who, while accepting that stress-inducing psychosocial processes will influence the magnitude of social pathologies, claims that the time lag between stress-related life events and the onset of many diseases is less than suggested by Brenner and his supporters. Eyer, reviewing medical studies, claims that the time lag is more likely to be under six months and that unemployment-related deaths might reasonably account for only a small fraction of the death rate variations associated with the business cycle. He suggests other possible influences on the rate of social pathology, which are more closely related to employment conditions experienced during the upswings of the business cycle. Those include stress-related situations such as overwork, lack of workers' solidarity, and the required increased worker mobility (i.e. break-up of community structure, family relations etc.).

Whether the controversy (*Lancet*, 1979) that has developed over the hypotheses of Brenner and Eyer is based on genuine differences between methods and assumptions that will eventually be resolved by further research or whether they are in fact investigating two distinct issues – the psychological consequences of unemployment and the psychological consequences of employment – is difficult to decide given the present empirical evidence, which is inevitably based on nation-wide indicators of social pathology and not on experiences influenced by an enormous variety of conditions.

Quite recently Brenner's data and arguments have been attacked from still another perspective. Winter (1981) argues, from historical data on infant mortality, that Brenner's short time-perspective leads to misleading, or at least grossly oversimplified results.

If this particular controversy is, therefore, of little help in comparing the psychological burden of employment with that of unemployment one looks to studies in which more attention is paid to concrete conditions.

Such a study has indeed been performed. Kasl (1979) in the U.S.A. has investigated the physical and psychological conditions of low-skilled blue-collar workers from the time when they were still employed but expected to be made redundant to four to six months after the plant closed down. This impressive study arrives at the conclusion that economic deprivation as well as the absence of their 'work-role' (largely measuring the absence of the categories of experience that employment enforces) is strongly felt on first becoming unemployed while there is hardly a change in the physiological indicators; at later periods in this investigation the sense of economic deprivation had intensified while the 'work-role' measures, that is the psychological consequences of unemployment, showed a positive adaptation to unemployment. In his conclusion Kasl suggests that the employment conditions of the low-skilled reduce their positive mental health so severely that 'the loss of the work-role ... among such disengaged workers may not be the trauma which facile generalisations from the "stressful life events" literature would seem to dictate' (p. 195).

While one cannot take exception to Kasl's findings nor to his comments on the employment conditions of the low-skilled, there are reasons why this study cannot settle the argument about whether unemployment presents greater stress than employment even under bad conditions. First, a period of four to six months is impressive in longitudinal research, given the difficulties of follow-up, but it is unfortunately relatively short in the perspective of the long-term unemployed. The time sequence of responses established in Marienthal, for example, extended over two or more years. While this process may differ fifty years later – indeed, where adequate redundancy payments are available the first shock experience may be replaced by or mixed with euphoric feelings – Kasl's investigation stopped at the second phase of the process.

Such considerations highlight once again the distinction between the absence of a category of experience and the quality of experience within that category. Whether or not some of the currently unemployed find their present condition less burdensome than their previous employment is a question that needs to be discussed in the light of more contemporary evidence. Before doing so another difficulty in assessing physical health and its possible deterioration through unemployment must be mentioned: at least in Great Britain there is among the unemployed a disproportionate percentage of disabled and not very healthy people. A recent survey of unemployed in several major cities (Smith, 1981) found that among white male unemployed 29% had some limiting disability (only 9% were registered as disabled, however); among minority group men the corresponding percentages were 16 and 5. It is possible that disablement led to unemployment, not the other way round. In addition the same survey found that 15% of the white group and fully 43% of the minority group judged themselves to be not too strong or in poor health. Once again the direction of causality cannot be determined from such studies; only longitudinal studies for prolonged time periods could settle the question of whether unemployment still has deleterious effects on nutrition and health, in spite of generally improved living conditions. No such work appears to be available at present.

Notwithstanding the difficulty of comparing the damaging effects of some employment conditions with those of unemployment in a general way, the comparison is inevitable in experience of unemployment.

47

That the intensity of a sense of deprivation, financially and psychologically, is greater in unemployment is already indicated by the fact that the overwhelming majority of the unemployed want a job. But since there exists such vast variety in previous job experiences it is not enough to leave it at that general level. Undoubtedly the comparison looks somewhat different for every individual affected, depending on a whole host of personal circumstances. Paraphrasing a famous formulation in the study of personality (Kluckhohn, Murray and Schneider, 1955), in some respects every unemployed is like every other unemployed (i.e. without a job); in some respects every unemployed is like some other unemployed (e.g. with similar previous jobs); and in some respects every unemployed is like no other unemployed (i.e. a unique individual). All these 'respects' raise legitimate issues. The identification of the five categories of compulsory experience that are no longer enforced in unemployment dealt with matters on the first, most general level that inevitably ignores differences in previous job experiences. The individual level is unmanageable for presentation other than in a few case histories; but there is the possibility of looking at the intermediate level, that is at specific groups whose employment and unemployment have broad similarities.

Four such groups deserve more detailed discussion: the first three – school-leavers, women, blacks – have not only particularly high unemployment rates but also special positions in the labour market. The fourth group, managers and professional personnel, is particularly relevant for understanding the meaning of jobs and of unemployment because the latter is for them most clearly divorced from the interfering influence of poverty, if not of financial worries. However, it must be said immediately that even though these four groups have often been singled out for discussion in the contemporary literature on unemployment, the comparison with previous job experiences is hardly ever made systematically and the psychological impact of unemployment is largely demonstrated by anecdotes and case material rather than through a systematic exploration of the relevant categories of experience that were identified from the studies during the depression in the thirties. Accordingly the following discussion of the employment and unemployment situation of these groups is, inevitably, less systematic than it should be, with a few notable exceptions.

The current situation of school-leavers must be viewed in the light of demographic facts. As a result of the 'baby boom', which in the U.K. reached a peak in 1964, a very much larger number reached the age of 16 in the current recession than did in the more prosperous 1960s. Casson (1979), for example, shows that the difference between the number of school-leavers available for employment and those reaching normal retirement age was 193,000 in 1977–8; for 1981–2 this difference is estimated to be 242,000. The surplus of school-leavers ready for employment is not limited to the U.K. and is reflected all over the industrialised world in the figures for youth unemployment. According to figures from the Organisation for Economic Co-operation and Development (Hawkins, 1979), in the seventies the ratio of unemployment rates of those under 25 years of age to adult rates was 9 in Italy, between 3 and 3.8 in Britain, Holland, Spain and Sweden and 1.7 in Belgium and West Germany. The situation is similar for the U.S.A. (Ginzberg, 1980) and for Australia (Brewer, 1975).

Demographic changes are one, but not the only reason for these high rates. Two other contrasting reasons are often cited: on the one hand it is said that the young have too high aspirations and hence shun the necessarily low-level jobs available for them; on the other hand, that school-leavers are so badly educated and so unwilling to work that they are virtually unemployable. Some research evidence is available for both these assertions. One current trend in the American labour force (Kanter, 1978) is a shift towards younger and more educated people; the same source also notes that dissatisfaction with blue-collar jobs is relatively higher in that group, indicating unfulfilled aspirations. The frequency of job changes by teenagers in the U.K. (Casson, 1979) is higher than that by young adults: resignations from the job because of dissatisfaction with it occur more often among male teenagers than among young adults. Since job satisfaction is, however, relatively high among the young in employment, there is here an indication that only a relatively small minority discover that their aspirations are not met by the jobs available to them. The crucial question yet to be answered is whether these findings are age-specific or whether today's dissatisfied teenage workers will be tomorrow's dissatisfied adult workers. Only longitudinal research could clinch the point.

A recent Australian study (Gurney, 1980), comparing employed and unemployed youngsters on data obtained just before leaving school and four months later, found signs of constructive psychosocial developments among those who had obtained a job but not among the unemployed, even though the two groups were fairly well matched to begin with. While the time interval is short, there is here an indication that not finding a job when leaving school may retard this group even as they advance in their chronological age.

Evidence for lack of aspirations with regard to work, already noticeable in the last few school years of some reluctant attenders, is provided not only by the mass media – though they undoubtedly lead to a widespread overestimate of the phenomenon – but also by systematic observations (e.g. Willis, 1977; and the Oldfield survey by the William Temple Foundation, 1980). Such studies present a frightening picture of a total mismatch between the content of compulsory education and the needs of a minority among school-children who, though not necessarily low in intelligence, are not academically inclined and often have a perfectly realistic view of their severely limited life chances, so that rebellion against authority and immediate gratification of every impulse become their life style to the despair of even their most understanding teachers. When unskilled casual employment was more plentiful, the Oldfield survey points out, such youngsters used to take a job for a month or two to earn the money for the next month of freedom to do as they liked. Now the opportunity for such casual acquaintances with the world of employment is severely reduced. The plight of these youngsters, truants in school and after, and of the neighbourhoods in which they try to lead their lives without hope and purpose, documented most often for the urban slums, is one of the most serious social consequences of large-scale unemployment. Black youngsters are at an even greater risk of joining their ranks. This one concludes from the fact that youth unemployment among blacks is about three times greater than for the total age group in the U.K., six times in the U.S.A.

To the extent that the psychological consequences of youth un-employment have been described, boredom, inactivity and lack of purpose are most often documented, while social contacts in that age group are apparently more easily maintained than among older un-employed. A West German study comparing 20–25-year-old un-employed men with older age groups found some significant differ-ences: fewer in the younger group found it embarrassing to talk to friends about their own unemployment and, somewhat surprisingly, more of them wondered whether they were unemployed through their own fault (Brinckmann, 1981, pp. 57–91). On the other hand an English study (Banks *et al.*, 1980) comparing the sense of general wellbeing of employed and unemployed school-leavers with adults in both positions found wellbeing much reduced in all unemployed, whether school-leavers or adults.

In one study unemployed school-leavers in Birmingham were interviewed three times in a period of 24 weeks (Stokes, 1981). The author found that initial despair and pessimism were during that period transformed into resignation and apathy, reminiscent of the process so often demonstrated in the thirties. But there is a difference. Resignation and apathy among these youngsters were indicated by hopelessness for the future and giving up looking for a job after repeated failures. But there was apparently no reduction in a diffused hostility against the community in the absence of a tangible target that could be blamed for their plight. While the interviews were conducted well before the recent youth riots, Stokes interprets the mood he observed as likely to lead to criminal behaviour.

The shortfall of jobs from which school-leavers suffer may in part be the result of the steadily growing number of women who enter the labour force, particularly married women. In 1951 they formed 21.7% of the British labour force; this percentage had risen to 47.9% in 1975. A very large proportion of all women in employment work in service industries; more than 40% work on a part-time basis, a percentage exceeded in Europe only in Denmark (42.4%), and much bigger than in other countries. Notwithstanding equal pay legislation the gross weekly earnings of full-time workers are still much higher for men than for women: in 1978 the U.K. average for men was £87.1, for women £56.4 (*Social Trends*, 1980). Similar trends have been noted in the U.S.A. (Kanter, 1978) and elsewhere. Women are still concentrated in the lower ranks in the occupational hierarchy, in the so-called 'female' jobs. In the U.S.A. white women have slightly gained as a proportion of college and university teachers, but for black women the proportion in professional employment has slightly dropped in the last twenty-five years.

These crude figures hardly indicate the very considerable changes in the climate of opinion with regard to the role of women in industrialised societies. Before the onset of the current recession these changes appeared to many to be irreversible. In view of the growth of unemployment and the spread of new technologies which reduce tthe demand for labour in 'female' occupations (clerical work and retail distribution) irreversibility is less certain, but the emancipatory struggle will undoubtedly continue. Once again it is not just the manifest financial consequences, important though they are for the vast majority of employed women, that constitute the benefits of employment, but its psychological meaning. Many women know from their own experiences or those of their mothers the depressive effect of being isolated without personal status and social identity, deprived of wider experiences than the highly emotionally charged family relations permit, and outside the communal purpose of the larger society, even though fully active in household work for the nuclear family.

Many married women prefer to work part-time for obvious reasons. A survey in the U.S.S.R. among women employed in factories, shops and restaurants spelled them out (Kuleshova and Mamontova, 1979): three-quarters of women with full-time jobs wanted to change either to a shorter day or shorter week, 62% because of their children, 14% wanted more time for themselves, 11% spoke of the pressure of domestic responsibilities, and 7% of poor health. (The same survey reported incidentally that the productivity of women put on four- or six-hour days rose by 15 to 30%.) The reluctance of managers to yield to the women's preference was explained by the difficulty this would present for the organisation of production. Such difficulties may be overcome if systematic job-sharing were introduced. This functions well enough where process-production or rush-orders make shift work necessary; there is no obvious reason why it should not function for half-day shifts. So far only sporadic anecdotal evidence is available on such arrangements in the U.K. (see e.g. McLoughlin, 1980).

That jobs, and by implication unemployment, have meaning for women beyond the income they provide has been demonstrated in many studies. In a large-scale recent interview survey in the U.S.A., for example (Nathanson, 1980), employment was identified as a source of self-esteem and social support, not of stress. What makes that study particularly interesting in the present context is its finding that these positive effects were strongest among women with little education who presumably held low-skilled jobs. The study also found, incidentally, that housewives reported a lower state of health than employed women. Once again, however, it is impossible to say whether lack of job influenced health or the other way round.

Such studies should nevertheless not disguise the fact that there are very many women in industrialised countries who by choice prefer to be housewives, notwithstanding the change in the cultural climate in this respect. And even if women prefer to have a job, unemployment hits them less hard than men psychologically speaking because an alternative is available to them in the return to the traditional role of housewife that provides some time structure, some sense of purpose, status and activity even though it offers little scope for wider social experiences. This lesser burden for unemployed women has been systematically investigated in West Germany (Brinkmann, 1981). For married unemployed women the financial problems are often less severe; fully 20% of them say they do not want to return to employment; much less often than men they tend to blame themselves for their unemployment; fewer women than men blame their unemployment for family conflicts and many more than men found it easy to talk to others about their situation. In only one area – missing the social contacts employment provided – many more women than men felt the psychological burden of unemployment.

The most comprehensive West German study of unemployed women (Heinemann, Röhrig and Stadie, 1980), based on a nation-wide quota sample that was interviewed twice with one half-year in between, concentrates in its analysis on the possibility that exists for large numbers of unemployed women to return to their more traditional role as housewives. If that were a frequent solution it might ease the unemployment situation in West Germany considerably, since Heinemann reports that women formed 55.3% of the registered unemployed in October 1978 (p. 61). *De facto*, however, only 17% of the women who were registered as unemployed at the time of the first interview identified themselves as housewives during the second. The long-time unemployed women in that study were found to have a less rational or explicit time structure, were more isolated in terms of having fewer friends and acquaintances, were more often resigned, and somewhat less emotionally stable than those who had jobs in both periods; fully 33% of these women said that unemployment was for them not a serious financial problem. All these findings are modified by other differences, that are extensively documented in the study.

For present purposes and in addition to the comparison with employed women, the psychological status of the unemployed compared with that of permanent housewives and with those who have changed into housewives is of interest. Half of the interviewed housewives wanted jobs because they felt isolated and longed to be among other people. Those housewives who had previously been employed had the least structured time experience and the narrowest time perspective, virtually excluding concern with the future. Those unemployed in both periods as well as those who had found employment again had considerably reduced their material demands on a job, thereby demonstrating that the retreat into the traditional female role was for them an undesirable choice. But this is different for women without qualifications: for many of them, in contrast to those with some qualifications, the role of housewife is a positive choice implying a reduction of working hours and of double duties.

Housewives at both periods, on the other hand, reported family conflicts least often; more of those who were unemployed in both periods or had returned to the traditional role indicated conflicts at home. These last two groups were also those who engaged mostly in passive leisure activities while those who returned to employment engaged most frequently in active pursuits even though they appeared to have less time for it. This demonstrates once again the impossibility of equating unemployment with leisure *per se*.

There are many more comparisons of various groups in these hefty two volumes, qualified by age, length of unemployment, family situation, status of partner, skill level, work motivation, political interest, perception of reasons for unemployment, etc. There is no question that all these factors enter into the experience of unemployment, of employment or of being a housewife. By the same token, however, such abundance of qualifications makes it hard indeed to see the wood for the trees. It remains to be seen whether the pressure of the women's liberation movement for economic independence of women or the restriction of the labour market will be the more powerful influence on the manner in which women exercise the relative freedom of choice they still have.

The problems of many blacks in employment and unemployment are heightened by racial prejudice and discrimination, so that their promotion chances are more limited, their unemployment rates higher (Smith, 1976). Being a minority among a white majority makes the acquisition of a clear sense of identity both more urgent and more difficult. For those not born in this country, differences in cultural background and language as well as inappropriate levels of skills intensify the problem of finding suitable employment. The experience in the U.S.A., however, clearly demonstrates that 200 years of black residence in a Western country is not enough to wipe out the disadvantages, though there are indications (Kanter, 1978) that the situation there is slowly improving in some aspects. Though a higher proportion of blacks than whites are unemployed, those who have jobs have a somewhat increased share in good jobs. The number of blacks in managerial positions has doubled, but is still only 4% of all managerial positions; also, black workers expressed increased job satisfaction at a time when that of whites showed no increase.

In the U.K. unemployment rates are higher for minority groups than for corresponding white groups; the rate is particularly high for young West Indians. The most recent comprehensive study of unemployment in racial minority groups (Smith, 1981) demonstrates, however, that race plays a smaller role in becoming unemployed than pre-existing inequalities:

> People at the lowest occupational levels are at least six times as likely to be unemployed as those at the highest levels ... People having low earnings within each occupational level ... even before they were out of work ... were earning no more than 60 per cent, on average, of the figure for manual workers generally. Also among those who are most at risk are people who have no qualifications, those who have a limiting disability, those with short service, and those who work in small establishments that are not unionised. (p. 148)

It is mostly because these risks are more frequent among racial minorities than among the white population, by and large not because of discrimination, that their unemployment rates are higher.

Against these solid and sober findings, which have not yet been recognised as widely as they deserve to be, stands the climate of opinion both among blacks and whites with its readiness to attribute unemployment to one's race or to the fact that some blacks have jobs while white people are unemployed. Incidents of racial hostility have increased in parallel with the rise in the overall unemployment rate, one of the most frightening examples of the social disintegration that results from the current shrinking of the labour market.

Managerial and professional unemployment is at present on the increase, though it hits of course, smaller numbers than manual unemployment. For this group redundancy payments are, as a rule, ample, and with tax refunds and personal savings few, if any, experience for some time a severe reduction in their standard of living, certainly not poverty. Evidence of their response to unemployment is, therefore, of special interest for the understanding of its psychological impact.

This group of unemployed, rather neglected in the earlier studies, is now receiving more attention. These are people with a normally high level of income who held high-level positions that carried high status in the community at large and enjoyed by and large more interesting jobs than manual workers, notwithstanding the psychological stresses that are often said to be associated with such positions, particularly industrial management. Their relatively limited number presents a serious difficulty for research: they are much more difficult to find and approach than the rest of the unemployed. Nonetheless a very large collection of case histories (Maurer, 1979) of unemployed persons in the U.S.A., many though not all of whom belong to this group, is available. This project in oral history graphically conveys every conceivable psychological response to unemployment among those for whom the fall came from a considerable height; but just because these case histories give such detailed insights into previous work history, and even personality, together with a detailed description of adaptation or its lack to unemployment, every case appears unique. However rich in impressions, however good as a source of hypotheses, no generalisations emerge from this material.

In England several, more systematic studies of unemployed managers and other professions have often tried to overcome the research difficulty of locating such people by approaching courses for unemployed managers run by the Training Services Division of the Manpower Services Commission. While this is probably the best one can do in going beyond individual cases, it inevitably introduces a bias into what we know about unemployed managers. These courses are, of course, voluntary; to avail oneself of such opportunities therefore implies a specific psychological stance, an effort at self-help. If there are unemployed high-status people who have yielded to despair or apathy and resignation, they will hardly be represented among the samples on which the studies depend. This possible psychological selectivity should be kept in mind when drawing conclusions from such research.

A corollary of the research setting in training courses is that the number of managers so studied is rather small in most studies; from a statistical point of view this is a disadvantage, but from the point of view of qualitative analysis a decided asset.

One such study (Fineman, 1979) found that eighteen out of twenty-five managers felt psychologically stressed by being unemployed, but the degree of stress was, of course, different for different individuals. The apparently reasonable assumption that a personality disposition to anxiety could fully account for this difference was shown to be too simple; a more important factor was an unemployed manager's degree of involvement with his previous job; those most involved suffered most in unemployment. As with everybody else, managers too felt understandably worse when their wives were unsympathetic and the job applications repeatedly failed.

Another study (Hartley, 1980) concentrated on the impact of unemployment on the self-esteem of managers and found no differences in that respect between a comparison group of employed managers and the unemployed on one statistical measure. But intensive interviews with a smaller sample showed that six unemployed managers had low self-esteem, eight defensively high self-esteem (putting on a 'brave face'), eight intermittently reduced self-esteem, and four high or moderate self-esteem. There is here an obvious discrepancy between the results for the larger group and the interview data. The former may lead to the conclusion that unemployment has not lowered the managers' general self-esteem; the interviews concentrating on the experience of unemployment suggest differently.

An even more recent study, largely concerned with establishing a sequence of responses as unemployment continued, reported that half the managers described their initial response as shock, for which the following is cited as an example (Swimburne, 1981, p. 99): 'The initial impact was absolute shock. A complete crushing of self respect and imagination'. There are similar examples in other studies (e.g. Hill, 1978). All one can conclude is that the evidence so far available on the point is not convincing either way. What these few studies do show is a much greater variety of responses, including some positive enjoyment of unemployment as a liberation from a confining job, than is the case with studies of other groups. Conspicuous in all these studies is the fact that financial hardship is hardly mentioned. It is, however, impossible to conclude with certainty that the greater variety of psychological responses is related to the relative lack of financial worries, even though the establishment of some such link was the major reason for singling out the managerial and professional unemployed.

This chapter began with one main question: given major social changes in the last half-century including a generally improved standard of living, is the psychological response to unemployment now different from what it was in the thirties? As was to be expected, the answer to this question is not simple, largely because the empirical evidence is still sporadic, not conclusive and rarely directly relevant to the psychological consequences of employment and their absence in unemployment.

There can be no doubt that unemployment now, as it did then, involves financial hardship for most individuals and their families. But while the unemployed half a century ago suffered absolute deprivation, the experience now is relative deprivation. There are not – at least not yet – reports on hunger and malnutrition among the unemployed; there are no beggars in the streets; the children of the unemployed have not been singled out for comment as being insufficiently fed and clad; dogs and cats are not disappearing from the streets to be served up as a meal. Nonetheless much of the current literature on unemployment emphasises the fact that despite significantly improved welfare provisions, the link between current unemployment and poverty is for many not broken, so that it seems impossible to disentangle psychological responses to the one from those to the other.

While it is impossible to compare systematically the intensity of the experience of poverty when it is absolute with the intensity when it is relative, one must assume that the former is more debilitating, if for no other reason than because it undermines the strength of the organism. This is why current psychological responses to unemployment can with somewhat greater confidence than in the past be attributed to the absence of a job not just to restricted finances.

For reasons given before it is as yet not possible to infer systematically from current empirical research what these responses are. On the other hand an analysis of employment as an institution makes it possible to specify some broad categories of experience, enforced on the overwhelming majority of those who participate in it: the imposition of a time structure, the enlargement of the scope of social experience into areas less emotionally charged than family life, participation in a collective purpose or effort, the assignment by virtue of employment of status and identity, and required regular activity. These categories of experience are not at the whim of a good or bad employer, but follow necessarily from the structural forms of modern employment. In that respect the structure of employment has remained unchanged not only since the thirties but certainly at least since the beginning of the industrial revolution. There are, of course, other institutions that enforce one or more of these categories on their participants; but none of them combines them all with as compelling a reason as earning one's living.

To the extent that these categories of experience have become a psychological requirement in modern life, the unemployed will suffer from their absence unless through their own deliberate efforts they have found alternative ways of satisfying these requirements. Even though no study has as yet systematically tested the psychological consequences of unemployment in these five categories which follow from the structure of employment (those who have conducted psychological studies have used either indicators of general wellbeing or have isolated one or the other category) there is some sporadic support in the material presented above for the experience of psychological deprivation in each of them among the unemployed.

The question arises whether these requirements are time- and culture-bound or are enduring needs of human beings. There are in the anthropological literature (e.g. Sahlins, 1974) examples of societies where employment as an institution does not exist; in some of them, privileged by favourable soil and climate, the need to work for a living is minimal. In these societies, however, the psychological functions of employment are met by rituals, religious and community practices, which provide the time experiences appropriate to that society, sharing of experience, recognition of collective purposes, a clear identity and the need for some activity. It is the manner in which time experiences are structured in industrialised societies through the ubiquity of employment conditions which forms the sharpest contrast to such societies, but the fact that institutions so radically different from those to which we have become accustomed provide otherwise analogous categories of psychological experiences lends support to the idea that enduring human needs are involved while at the same time demonstrating the variability of institutions that can satisfy such needs.

Further support for the notion that these needs are more enduring than the institutions that satisfy them at a given time – and by implication support for the psychological deprivation of the unemployed – comes from Freud's psychological thought. His aphorism that work is man's strongest tie to reality (Freud, 1930) and its reversal – unemployment loosens man's grip on reality – must be understood within his general conception of human needs. He postulates that the early domination of the pleasure principle, that is the search for immediate gratification, is in the course of normal development modified by a growing ability to perceive reality and delay gratification accordingly. The normal person, if reality is hostile, tries to change it; the neurotic withdraws from it; the psychotic fantasises an alternative reality in which the pleasure principle dominates again as in infancy. The pleasure and the reality principle are thus complementary, not opposed to each other. That the reality tie requires continuous reinforcement is demonstrated in experiments in which people are immersed in a water tank and deprived of all stimulations from the environment; after only a few hours in this condition they begin to hallucinate. Donald Hebb who conducted these experiments and whose theoretical stance is opposed to that of Freud, nevertheless confirms the damaging effect of cutting ties with reality; indeed he postulated (Hebb and Thompson, 1954) that the psychological function of the social environment was to protect man through institutional arrangements from being swamped by extreme emotionality.

Heinz Hartmann (1964) has elaborated the Freudian assumptions by distinguishing three ways in which we continuously keep in touch with reality: by inferring from observable consequences of activities that external objects really are or behave as we think they should; by sharing with others 'conventional' or 'socialised' knowledge of reality; and by the testimony of our perceptions, that is by the world of immediate experience. Employment as an institution provides compelling opportunities to engage in continuous reality testing in all three ways.

Now it would be foolish indeed to maintain that the unemployed have lost all opportunity for keeping in touch with reality; on the contrary, they know all too well the bitter reality of their economic situation, they have not abandoned their shared conventional knowledge of the world and every one of their actions, casual or not, confirms the existence of the external world. In all these respects, however, the opportunities are severely restricted in scope; their grip on reality is not lost but loosened; for most of them it is still strong enough to know what they are missing when they complain about boredom, being on the scrap-heap and isolated.

From such considerations I conclude that the psychological needs met by employment are probably deeper and more enduring than the institutional arrangements to which we have become accustomed as satisfying them. But these institutional arrangements are so intricately interwoven with the very nature of modern societies that they themselves are likely to endure for a long time, certainly for longer than it makes sense to look ahead.

A more immediate issue is the nature of the reality that faces those who are tied to it by employment. That not all is well in the world of employment is beyond question. Though it provides the required categories of experience, their quality is on occasion so deplorable that many commentators regard unemployment (with adequate financial support) preferable to such employment. For reasons spelled out before, I cannot agree with this, but this does not imply an acceptance of current employment conditions. Indeed, it is another unfortunate consequence of mass unemployment that it absorbs the centre of the public debate and pushes to the periphery concern with the problems of employment. To consider them in some detail is the task of the next chapter.

5

Can employment be humanised?

Not all the unemployed live in poverty; not all the poor are unemployed. Wage-earners on the lowest level with large families, the disabled and one-parent families constitute a significant proportion of the poor in Britain and elsewhere. To raise the income level of these people in employment is the necessary first step towards humanisation. But the vast majority of those in regular employment are not poor. It is to the conditions under which they make their living that the growing demands for improvement in the quality of working life are directed. Even on the assumption that the categories of experience provided by employment convey more psychological support than unemployment, the quality of these experiences may present psychological burdens of its own kind.

A one-sided glance at the research literature may make light of this. After all there are many systematic sample surveys, conducted over decades in many countries, that demonstrate that the vast majority of those with jobs – as a rule, around 70%, but even 80% and 90% have been found – declare themselves satisfied with their jobs. These results cannot be brushed aside as methodological artifacts. They do mean something, the question is: what? It has been suggested before that at a minimal level these data mean that any employment is better than unemployment, psychologically and financially; others agree (e.g. Westley, 1979). But surely this is not enough. There are on all levels of the industrial hierarchy people who derive genuine satisfaction from what they are doing and from the conditions under which they are employed – albeit more so on the higher than the lower levels – as well as people on all levels who are deeply frustrated in one or both respects. Individual differences of course play their role. It is therefore unlikely that for the great mass of employees, particularly for the unskilled who express satisfaction relatively least often, 'one correct managerial strategy [can be designed] to influence employee satisfaction which works for all persons, across all situations, and at all times' (Katz and Van Maanen, 1977, p. 470). Granted; but managerial strategies are in any case only one among several aspects which have been diagnosed as major reasons for frustration in employment.

Further analysis of survey data and many other studies have shown that overall satisfaction or dissatisfaction is the resultant of weighting against each other positive and negative features of the job, not of using the income it provides as the only yardstick. Indeed, income is taken so much for granted as the most obvious reason for holding a job that it is hardly ever mentioned in the first place to explain the level of overall satisfaction. But thinking about the humanisation of employment must go beyond what people are willing and able to say in answer to an interviewer's question. The arguments of those who regard employment as an institution as inevitably degrading and who sense widespread and growing alienation everywhere, even in the most privileged occupations in modern societies, the professions (Pym, 1975; Kumar, 1978), include the idea that current conditions have had so severe a corrupting influence on those in employment that the employed have passively adjusted and lost their ability even to imagine genuine work satisfaction under humane conditions. This is not only an ideological stance but at least for the lowest level of required skills supported by some evidence mentioned in the previous chapter; psychologically damaging consequences of some employment conditions have been demonstrated to exist by by-passing the direct awareness of those so affected. The low score on mental health among unskilled car-workers, for example (Kornhauser, 1958), can well go together with these workers saying that they are satisfied with their jobs.

Those concerned with the humanisation of work are thus confronted with a moral dilemma: if by their own standards some conditions of employment are judged to be dehumanising while those concerned express themselves as satisfied with their lot, by what right can the former impose their standards on the latter, particularly if whatever level of adjustment to their situation satisfied job-holders have attained must be undermined to get their co-operation for change? There is some evidence that highlights the dilemma: a Dutch study (Hofstede, 1979) investigated the values held by humanisers and those on the shopfloor and came to the conclusion that the humanisation of employment is advocated by the former but has little bearing on the values of the latter. Marxists deal with this issue by their concept of 'false consciousness' – 'false' in the sense that it contradicts what the theory stipulates people should be conscious of – and therefore have no qualms about trying to put people's consciousness right even if it destroys their satisfaction. To be sure, this is one way of solving the moral dilemma, but it is not to everybody's taste. Most people concerned with the humanisation of work would insist on some evidence of more positive consequences, that is on evidence that enduring frustrations in some employment situations can be deliberately eliminated.

Sporadic examples of the nature of these frustrations have already been given in previous chapters; a more systematic presentation must examine the causes of frustration that have been identified. There are three major causes: the general structure of industrialised societies, the organisational structure of enterprises, and the nature of the tasks in which employees are engaged.

The Marxist literature maintains that the negative consequences of employment and unemployment are the result of capitalism. This view is hard to test because none of the existing socialist societies could or does claim to have completed the transition from capitalism to Marx's concept of socialism; none, certainly, has made the jump from the realm of necessity into the realm of freedom, nothwithstanding common ownership of the means of production. Nonetheless societies based on such common ownership are radically different from Western capitalism, so that comparisons may be illuminating. While data from planned economies are sparse, some information is available.

For example, a West German review of East German research on attitudes to work quotes some startling figures. In 1968 only 50% of women workers on the assembly line felt content during and after work; in 1973 this percentage had dropped to 20. In 1968 very few of those women wanted different jobs; in 1973 it was 60% (Temmen, 1979).

Soviet Russia guarantees in its constitution the right to work, but the common ownership of the means of production does not seem to have eliminated their labour problems. Professor Gavrich Popov, economist from Moscow State University, is reported to argue in an article in

Pravda that 'Only by creating a pool of temporarily unemployed workers . . . will the state be able to reduce overmanning in industry . . . the threat of dismissal will galvanise lazy workers into greater productivity and induce them to respect their place of work a little more' (Binyon, 1981).

In an opinion poll in Poland conducted in September 1980 (Kurczewski, 1981) people were asked about their expectations for the future; well over 70% expressed the hope that workers would acquire the power to run enterprises, thereby indicating their dissatisfaction with current conditions. Given Poland's economic situation it is interesting to note that this is a somewhat higher percentage than that expecting and hoping for improvements in the provision of food.

As far as one can judge employment conditions in Yugoslavia, rightly famous for its experiments in industrial organisation and different from other communist countries, the aims of eliminating frustrating employment conditions have not been realised so far. In an article sympathetic to the Yugoslav experiment in self-management the authors (Baumgartner, Burns and Seculic, 1979, p. 102) conclude: 'The means of production are not privately owned and sanctions based on property concepts are not available to management. Nevertheless, the social division of labour . . . and the technologies utilised . . . operate to develop and reproduce unequal power and control relationships and uneven accumulation of knowledge, capabilities and social linkages among actors engaged in production'. While they do not name alienation, the causes and consequences of unequal power they list are much the same as those that under capitalism are said to lead to alienation. Evan (1977) discusses several other studies of Yugoslav conditions; they all arrive at the same conclusion.

Limited though this evidence is, it appears to indicate similarities rather than differences when the problems of employment under capitalism are compared with those under communism.

If the broad context of social organisation has thus not been demonstrated – at least not yet – to eliminate the problems of employment, it is possible that narrower contextual factors immediately available to direct experience might mitigate them. This one would expect in any case from one of the few valid generalisations of social psychology: direct experience is a stronger factor in shaping actions and behaviour and a better transmitter of information than verbal representations outside the social context to which they refer. Both in communist and capitalist countries conditions vary, of course, enormously from enterprise to enterprise; but until quite recently the internal organisation based on a strict authority structure has in the majority of enterprises hardly changed in this century: 'organisations are based on concepts of scientific management . . . proposed at a time when the average length of schooling of the work force was three years' (Davis, 1977, p. 262).

Throughout this century there were, of course, exceptions to this rule, but by and large concern with organisational changes intended to affect the experience of employment gathered some momentum only after the Second World War during the period of relatively full employment. Some social scientists and some industrialists (hardly ever trade unionists in the U.S.A. and U.K., though these were actively involved in Scandinavian countries) began to co-operate in quasi-experimental studies of the impact of deliberate organisational change on workers' morale, that is on the quality of experiences in employment. The rationale underlying these early studies was highlighted by Elton Mayo (1945) based on the Hawthorne studies (Roethlisberger and Dickson, 1939). These famous studies demonstrated that improvement of productivity was less a function of the physical, more of the social environment; when people were treated not as pairs of hands but as persons, when their spontaneous group formation on the shop-floor was recognised, their productivity rose, absenteeism and labour turnover fell. The 'human relations' approach to employment problems was born. While it has some ameliorations of employment conditions to its credit, two things should be noted: first, these studies have often been criticised on ideological grounds (Landsberger, 1958, has summarised these criticisms and refuted some); and second, the positive experiences of the labour force were regarded as a means to the end of higher productivity, not as an end in itself. There is, of course, nothing wrong with productivity as an end in itself; but there is something wrong with regarding the quality of life in employment as a legitimate concern only if it serves productivity and other economic aims. In an ideal world the two ends would invariably reinforce each other. In the world as it is this is sometimes but not always the case, and the conditions under which it is, have so far escaped specification, notwithstanding a very rich research literature on the subject.

Another well-known early study confirmed the mutual reinforcement of productivity and morale. Coch and French (1948) experimented in a factory with different modes of introducing organisational change. One group of employees participated fully as a group in deciding how a required technical change should be implemented; this group was compared with two others, one that had chosen representatives to the decision-making body and one without any form of participation. Their results were dramatic: only the fully participating group adapted immediately to change and showed increases both in morale and output. Many replications and variations of this experiment followed; the results are equivocal. Many but not all studies confirm the positive effect of direct participation on morale, but a considerable number could detect no impact on productivity or found occasionally even a negative impact (Powell and Schlacter, 1976). And, once again, the methodology of the early seminal experiment has been severely criticised (Gardner, 1977).

One carefully designed English study (Lischeron and Wall, 1975) discovered that the form of participation that was experimentally introduced was popular with employees and managers, was regarded as worth while by the vast majority and improved the relations between workers and their managers, but did not increase satisfaction with the organisation, pay, opportunities for promotion, the job itself, immediate superiors or co-workers. The authors soberly conclude 'that the empirical evidence has become distorted by value orientations. Because investigators wish to believe that participative approaches to organisational management are desirable they are too eager to document that proposition from available evidence' (p. 882). The emphasis in this statement on the intrusion of ideological stances into the interpretation of empirical evidence is justified. But it would be wrong to infer from it and from the inconsistency of research results in this area that the psychological value of participation in decision-making has thereby been discredited; the expectation, however, that it will increase satisfaction in all job aspects must be dropped. In this particular study neither pay nor promotion opportunities nor other aspects of the job were apparently changed through participation; there was therefore no conceivable reason for the employees to change their minds about them.

The positive impact that was documented in this study – participation is popular and worth while, relations between employees and management improved – as well as the lack of impact on satisfaction with specific employment features, raises the more general question of what can and what cannot be reasonably expected from participative arrangements in employment.

Such participation can take various forms (Jahoda, 1979). In West Germany there are legal provisions for worker directors, the *Mitbestimmungsrecht*, that guarantee participation of representatives of the labour force in top-level policy decisions. In Britain similar arrangements were suggested by a public Committee of Inquiry (Bullock, 1977), but not implemented in view of strong opposition from many industrialists and some trade unionists who rejected the anticipated interference of such arrangements either with the structure of industrial power and authority or with loyalty to the basic principles of unionism. The background to this Inquiry and the political conflict around it have been fully analysed by Elliott (1978). Nonetheless there are some British enterprises that have on a voluntary basis in private industry and by political arrangements in some nationalised industries instituted participation on several levels of the industrial hierarchy, including board membership by representatives of the workforce.

To the best of my knowledge the impact of labour force representation, where it exists, on the content of top-level economic policy has as yet not been documented. This is a curious omission by proponents as well as adversaries in the debate about industrial democracy in an area otherwise dominated by economic thought. It remains an urgent task for the future to supply this missing evidence that could lend more substance to this largely ideological struggle.

Fortunately – from the point of view of this book – the debate is more outspoken and the evidence more plentiful on the social-psychological meaning of participation at lower levels. The Bullock Report put great emphasis on participation at all levels, arguing that participation at the top makes direct participation at lower levels more meaningful. Because of the primacy of immediate experience it stands to reason that power sharing at the top in long-term policy decisions will not immediately affect attitudes on the shopfloor; nor will participation in decisions on the shopfloor have lasting psychological effects if they can be countermanded from the top. From all that is known about the quality of experiences on the job it is on the lowest level of the industrial or bureaucratic hierarchy that traditional organisational forms are often experienced as oppressive. In contrast to the lack of time structure in the lives of the unemployed, time here is often too rigidly structured in minute periods in repetitive activities; there is no scope for initiative or self-determination; the purposes of activities and the manner in which they have to be carried out are often obscure; many regulations emphasise the low status of the employed that is heightened by a built-in mistrust of the ability of the employed to use judgement. What can participation in decision-making achieve in such a situation?

There are two basic human needs that are left unmet by such conditions. The first of these is the universal need to understand the world, to make sense of events, to see through the baffling diversity of appearances to the underlying meaning of it all. Two of the thinkers who have shaped the intellectual climate of our times, Marx and Freud, have – at least in part – attained their enormous influence because they both appeal to this need to understand, to make visible the invisible: Freud by explaining man to himself, Marx by explaining society to men. Confirmation of this universal search for meaning comes from other areas too. All perceptions of the external world around us are governed by it. The clearer and simpler an external object is, the closer will perception reflect its actual attributes; if the object is opaque, complex or ambiguous, the perceiver will impose on it a meaning that stems from predispositions and past life experiences. Such imposed meaning may have little, if anything, to do with actual realities. The universality of the search for meaning is further demonstrated by the fact that there is no known culture, past or present, developed or less developed, without a way of explaining why things are as they are. The very fact that these explanations are so diverse indicates that the need to understand the world around us will never be satisfied once and for all. But even if the eternal questions are unanswerable, people strive to understand the events of daily life and resent arrangements that defy their understanding.

Traditional industrial organisation ignores this need of employees; participation in decision-making promises to meet it. It increases the visibility of rules and regulations by providing opportunity to question and shape them; it undermines depersonalisation and anonymity; it will not automatically increase productivity. If what is made more visible by direct participation is detrimental to the participants, increased effort and output could hardly be expected.

The second need that could be met by participation is the need for some degree of personal control over one's immediate environment. In this respect the report to the U.S. Department of Health, Education and Welfare, entitled *Work in America*, recognised what is needed in 1973: 'What workers want most, as more than 100 studies in the past 20 years show, is to become masters of their immediate environment and to feel that their work and they themselves are important' (D.H.E.W., 1973).

Shopfloor observations from the Hawthorne studies onwards have demonstrated how much ingenuity manual workers in traditional organisations invest in efforts at exercising personal control, and not only when the work-study expert tries to fix rates for a job with stopwatch in hand. People on piecework have been observed working at full speed for a while in order to relax, have a smoke and generally take it easy afterwards (e.g. Lupton, 1963; Klein, 1964). Of course, organised employment could never provide the opportunity for maximal personal control that independent craftsmen and some professionals and artists enjoy. But not everybody can function optimally without some support from external requirements. What is needed in employment is an appropriate mixture of personal and external control, and not only on the conveyor belt. Participation in decision-making about the immediate job structure and environment extends the scope for personal control of rules and regulations that are otherwise experienced as autocratically imposed.

These two human needs – that for understanding and that for a certain amount of personal control – are sometimes met without formal arrangements, perhaps more often in small enterprises than in large ones. But even in some large ones some shop stewards have interpreted their role so as to meet them. An extension of these practices could humanise other job experiences. But not only do some managers and some trade unionists not see it that way, there is also some evidence to the effect that many shopfloor workers, particularly the unskilled, do not actually want it. Even in Yugoslavia where the entire power of the state is committed to de-centralised participation in all its industries on all levels such resistance appears. While the works councils there are intended to consist of all grades of workers, while most of them were so constituted to begin with, after some time manual workers tended to drop out, to be replaced or not to stand for re-election. The Yugoslav government has periodically introduced new measures to rectify this, but the emergence of experts as the real decision-makers seems hard to control.

There exists a systematic study of the actual practice of industrial participation in Yugoslavia (Mozina, Jerovsek, Tannenbaum and Likert, 1976) that deserves mention. The authors identified ten pairs of enterprises each matched for products, technology, capital investment, etc., but differing in performance. The firms with higher achievement were found to be closer to participative management than those with lesser achievements. The authors go out of their way to emphasise that a power structure and strong leadership must exist and that power was *not* more equally spread in the more successful firms. They explain the difference between participation and power sharing somewhat surprisingly by stating that decisions arrived at by participative arrangements are not necessarily carried out.

This could encourage the cynical interpretation that such participation is sham. However, the purpose of participation was defined in that study as enabling members of an enterprise to 'feel a sense of personal worth and importance'; if that aim can genuinely be achieved – as it apparently was – participation even without power sharing is a step towards humanisation of employment.

What one takes from these and other studies is that it is neither an easy nor a uniformly popular step to introduce participatory arrangements; it meets with least enthusiasm where it is apparently most needed; it is occasionally introduced with the expectation that it will lead to greater economic efficiency, an expectation that is more often frustrated than fulfilled. And yet it has the potential of humanising employment conditions by meeting the need to understand, and providing the possibility of exercising some control over one's immediate environment. Increased understanding may, however, only lead to the recognition that other organisational deficiencies exist and that the control over one's immediate environment is limited indeed. This is why in such cases it does not necessarily lead to increased productivity nor to reduction in alienation.

Over the two centuries of capitalism in the West it is not only revolutionaries who have regarded labouring for somebody else's profit as the crux of the matter but also idealistic radical reformers who have accordingly experimented with enterprises based on common ownership by the entire workforce, producer co-operatives and profit sharing schemes. Many of such employee-owned enterprises have gone bankrupt; some have survived; hardly any have been studied systematically. While their economic outcome is relatively well documented the reasons for their success or failure are not so well understood; and the impact of such arrangements on motivation, satisfaction and dissatisfaction of those in otherwise alienating jobs has hardly been explored. We simply do not know whether monotonous jobs can be turned into satisfying work through the knowledge that one is working for one's own profit. The parallel with the Yugoslav form of industrial organisation is obvious but leaves the answer ambiguous. There are some hints from journalists' reports on the perhaps most successful producer co-operative, Mondragon in the Basque country, to the effect that the size of such an enterprise had much to do with the degree of employees' morale. Apparently Mondragon experienced one strike in a factory employing 5,000 people. Having analysed this event they arrived at the conclusion not to let any single enterprise grow beyond 2,000. So far no obvious further outbreaks of overt dissatisfaction seem to have occurred.

In view of the sparsity of social-psychological knowledge about such organisations one American exploratory study of employee ownership is worth mentioning. Long (1978) studied a medium-sized trucking firm six months after 70% of the employees had bought the firm's stock that had previously belonged to a large corporation. As in Mondragon employees had to buy themselves into the enterprise; but in contrast to Mondragon 30% of the employees were not stockholders. From a research point of view this was an almost ideal situation, permitting comparison between those who had acquired the rights to profits and to voting for representatives on the board of directors on which management and representatives of the employees sat and those who had not. The results in economic and in human terms were encouraging: labour turnover dropped by 30%, damage claims for improper handling by 60%. Productivity increased and the firm that had made losses in the preceding five years was set for profit in the first year of co-ownership. On the psychological side more than 80% of the employees reported increased satisfaction, about two-thirds said their own efforts had increased and the same proportion felt this also about their colleagues. It is interesting to note that the increase in satisfaction was much higher than the increase in participation in decision-making – only about half the employees felt they were more involved in such participation than before. All these improvements were more pronounced for stock-holders than for the rest.

Unfortunately the study does not report what the financial gain for individual employees was. The expectation of material rewards undoubtedly played a significant role in the various improvements, but it was not the only factor. Co-ownership does not result in mechanical equality of rewards and duties; but it could lead to an equality of commitment to a common purpose among all engaged in an enterprise, with economic and psychological benefits for all. It could be the economic infra-structure on which participation in decision-making may build more safely than in situations where profit is not shared with employees but distributed elsewhere.

There are anecdotal reports of similar arrangements from many countries; their systematic investigation remains a task for the future. These relatively small-scale efforts to change the industrial hierarchy in one materially and psychologically significant aspect are different from common ownership of the means of production as in Soviet Russia and from nationalisation of some industries in Western mixed economies because they avoid mediation by the state bureaucracy and remain with their assets and liabilities within the scope of direct personal experience of the labour force. In that respect they have more similarity with Yugoslavian industrial organisation where wages vary according to the profits of single enterprises. Social-psychological research there has, however, concentrated on participation without including the effects on material rewards. It is just possible that in practice as well as in research the concentration on the potential benefits of participation *per se* has resulted in ambiguities because it ignored the making-a-living aspect of employment.

An approach to the problems of the immediate working environment that includes participation in decision-making but is not limited to it has been developed by the Tavistock Institute of Human Relations: socio-technical systems analysis. As the name indicates it deals with the entire enterprise as a system, recognising formally what practitioners are inevitably aware of, namely that in employment human experiences, organisational structures and technical processes continuously interact so that none can be fully understood unless the other components are simultaneously considered. Thus it defines the topic of research in industry as the entire system – people, organisation, technology – established to perform a central task.

If, in this statement, socio-technical analysis appears to do no more than catch up with common-sense, it is appropriate to point out that such common-sense is not yet applied by all practitioners nor by all researchers. But socio-technical systems analysis has actually proceeded beyond common-sense in clarifying some basic concepts, arriving at some empirical generalisations and demonstrating in research that this approach can significantly increase the understanding of employment situations and indicate where and how organisational change should be implemented.

For present purposes the most relevant concept is 'central task'. The most relevant empirical generalisations are that the problems on one level of organisation depend more frequently on those at a higher level, not vice versa; and that there are several possible forms of social organisation that go with a given technology, so that there is a possibility for choice and experiment. The most general formulation of the central task of employment is the provision of goods and services. In practice this task is often further specified as the production of goods and services for the purpose of making profit on investment. The implicit argument of this book is for a further addition to this definition of central task, namely that the pursuit of the purpose be limited by consideration for the physical and psychological wellbeing of all employees. The first generalisation mentioned above provides support for the Bullock Report's insistence on participation also at top levels, the second for experimenting with change.

The famous, by now classical study in which these ideas were fully developed for the first time was a study of coal-mining (Trist and Bamford, 1951). There it was shown from an analysis of the requirements of the technology that the traditional deployment of miners was technologically not optimal when new methods of coal-getting were introduced and that this was one of the reasons for frustration among them. A change in social organisation for a better fit with the new technology led to increased productivity and increased morale.

A few years later another member of the Tavistock Institute (Rice,

1958) used this same approach for reorganising a textile mill in Ahmedabad, India, with remarkable success in output and satisfaction. The basic idea was to reorganise a large work-shed with 560 looms into small semi-autonomous workgroups which received a group bonus for quantity and quality of production that increased their earnings considerably. Rice remained a consultant to the mill for several years, and maintained the new organisation and its successful performance. Seventeen years after the first reorganisation Miller (1975) did a follow-up study. Much had changed in products, production process, market conditions, personnel, managerial style and concerns. Only in one shed had the organisation into semi-autonomous groups been maintained and, with it, the improvements Rice had noticed; in others changes in product and personnel and increased pressure from management had led to a return to more traditional forms of organisation with reduced efficiency and increase in damaged or faulty products. Miller's meticulous analysis of possible reasons for success and failure in the long term does not lead to simple conclusions beyond saying that it is easier to improve a very poor fit between technology and social organisations than to maintain such improvements over many years when new people are confronted with new pressures.

Since then the socio-technical systems approach has been used in many countries and many industries (e.g. Klein, 1976*b*). While it has not lost its power as an analytical tool for understanding the employment situation, the dramatic early successes in introducing socio-technical change have not always been repeated. This does not invalidate the approach – that industrial systems are not closed but open to the surrounding historical, social and cultural influences has always been emphasised in socio-technical analysis. It does highlight the peculiar character of social-psychological results: in their concrete bearing on human experiences their validity is inevitably time- and culture-bound. If some results endure across time and space, as seems to be the case for the psychological experience of unemployment, this cannot be taken for granted but must be established as a result, not treated as a foregone conclusion from previous research. In the social sciences, very much in contrast to the natural sciences, concepts, ideas and approaches have a somewhat longer life-expectancy than the phenomena with which they deal.

Within a socio-technical approach, though without its emphasis on

75

experimenting with organisational change, Joan Woodward (1965) distinguished mass production, flow production and batch production in the 100-odd firms she studied, and could demonstrate significant differences in the experiences of people so employed, particularly with regard to industrial relations. She found industrial relations considerably more satisfactory in flow production when the rhythm of work depended on an ongoing sophisticated process than in mass production when this was determined by human beings, foremen and supervisors, who set the speed of the conveyor belt. The skills required in process production are perceptual and judgemental, in mass production manual; in the former the process-worker is in control, in the latter he is being controlled. It is the contrast between being employed as a person rather than a pair of hands. The latter condition arouses the greatest frustration. Not surprisingly the few documented examples of industrial sabotage involving deliberate destruction of machinery come from car-workers on the conveyor belt (Brown, 1977).

Recognition of the psychologically destructive impact of this form of work organisation lay behind the famous experiments in the Swedish car industry, based on small groups containing people with all the skills required to produce the final product, but there are conflicting reports about the economic viability of this socio-technical approach. Kanter (1978) mentions a month-long visit by six American car-workers to this Swedish experiment; they were unimpressed or even antagonistic to it. This is in line with the views of an experienced American labour lawyer who asserts unhesitatingly that American workers are simply not concerned with participation in any form. He knows the claims made for industrial participation which, he says, 'is urged as a solution to such widespread problems of industrial society as worker alienation, low productivity, industrial conflict and political unrest. It is also said to contribute to effective management and productive efficiency; ... In the United States labor organisations have not only failed to show interest in co-determination but they are hostile to such ideas' (Dunlop, 1978).

Even if the view that Dunlop attributes to American unions is as universal as he claims, it is certainly not unchangeable. Resistances against humanisation efforts by those whom they are meant to benefit are widespread in many countries, as has been shown. While most relevant studies have not gone beyond demonstrating this ineluctable fact, there is at least one exciting and promising major action research project now in progress at the University of Bremen (Leithäuser, 1979) that has as its major aim the analysis of these resistances and the development of measures to counteract them in concrete industrial work situations.

Whatever the immediate organisational context in which a job is performed, the activity itself that a person is required to carry out must also affect, of course, the psychological meaning of the job. It is all too easy for social scientists whose own work is challenging and not routinised to assume that everybody in monotonous and repetitive jobs would resent them as much as they would. Just as not everybody in the labour force wants to participate in decision-making, so not everybody resents repetitive work. Many women, for example, particularly those in part-time industrial employment, do not appear to object to such occupations if physical and wage conditions are adequate. This is also the case for the employment experience of handicapped people (Tizard and Anderson, 1979) and must be the case, one is inclined to assume, for some others in the labour force. Whether or not an activity is 'soul-destroying' is a question of the match between individual abilities and individual demands on the one hand and the nature of the job on the other.

Even though the nature of some jobs reduces individual abilities and levels of aspiration, as previously indicated (Kornhauser, 1965; Kasl, 1979), the fact of the matter appears to be that many employees have not reduced their aspirations but experience a mismatch between what they can do and what they have to do and feel frustrated by being underused and not challenged by the activity they have to carry out. At least from the beginning of the century onwards there is sporadic evidence that the progressive division of labour, accompanied by a progressive rise in levels of education, has increased in many the sense of being underused and resulted in frustration and resentment, even when financial rewards were not a cause for complaint. The resentment of labourers against Frederick Taylor after he had increased their earnings significantly is one example; in mid-century a study of assembly-line workers (Guest, 1952) discovered that a large majority of men were unhappy about the repetitiveness of their jobs and the lack of opportunity to develop skills, in spite of high earnings.

The idea that alienation is increasing because the activities people have to carry out in their jobs are becoming less and less challenging goes back at least to Adam Smith, but it was, of course, Karl Marx who made it central to his critique of capitalism. For Marx alienation was the result of private ownership of the means of production and of the progressive division of labour. Many social scientists have attempted to convert the idea of alienation into indices for application in empirical research. One of the most interesting of these attempts is based on a representative sample of the U.S. population in civilian employment (Kohn, 1976). This methodologically and intellectually highly sophisticated study, properly qualified for a given time in a given country, arrives at the conclusion that being or not being an owner is relatively unimportant as a source of feeling powerless, self-estranged or normless (Kohn's indicators of alienation); even less important, he found, was the level of bureaucratisation of an enterprise. The dominant source of alienation was the lack of opportunity to use self-direction in the actual task on the job; where there were close supervision, routinised tasks, and simple, unchallenging activities alienation was most pronounced.

In a subsequent publication (Kohn and Schooler, 1981) reporting a re-assessment after ten years of both the complexity of a task and the intellectual flexibility of the workers the authors found a remarkably strong impact of the task on personal flexibility. Workers who had been assigned to complex tasks tended to demonstrate increased intellectual flexibility, workers on simple tasks reduced flexibility compared with their scores ten years before. The implication is that the nature of the job makes a lasting impact on individuals which affects not only their functioning in employment but their total personality.

To the extent that these findings can be generalised one must accept the fact that many now in the most routinised jobs have lost what it takes to fill more challenging positions even if they were available. To reduce their number will be a slow and long process, depending on the improvement of the educational institutions for the young and for adults. There are, however, many who have not lost their ability and desire for more interesting jobs but find themselves in activities that demand less than they can give. It is the alienation of these employees who have not – at least not yet – been psychologically damaged by routinised work that can be avoided or undone in the shorter run by appropriate action.

The research unit at Phillips in Eindhoven, for example, aimed at an 'objective' assessment of the match or mismatch between their employees' capacity and the demands of their jobs (den Hertog, 1976) by testing the manual workers for various skill levels and comparing these for each worker with a systematic analysis of the skill requirements of his job. A large excess of underused skill emerged. The study also demonstrated that labour turnover was very high when people with high capacity were assigned to simple jobs. In view of this situation job enlargement and enrichment measures were introduced and met with considerable success.

There exist many studies of the impact of job enrichment and enlargement (e.g. Orpen, 1979). Typically they show improved attitudes to jobs that were more varied and more under the control of an individual, but not increased productivity. So Orpen found after six months during which employees had been working under enriched conditions that satisfaction, involvement and motivation had increased, absenteeism and turnover decreased; but there was little impact on output and performance. Such results parallel the impact of participation in decision-making, which is, indeed, a form of job enrichment. Strange bedfellows – some employers and most revolutionaries – therefore reject such efforts at humanisation, albeit for different reasons: employers because it does not 'pay', revolutionaries because such employment may constitute another 'opium for the people'. Both are prepared to sacrifice the psychological wellbeing of people to their own interests.

The idea of fitting the job to the worker has a psychological and a physiological component. The latter is the subject matter of ergonomics, which is concerned with designing equipment so as to be optimally suited to the attributes of the human organism. Ergonomic studies have made many important contributions to easing the physical stress in a large variety of jobs. The transfer of the basic ergonomic idea into the field of psychology is of more recent origin and meets with considerable difficulty. While it is justifiable to fit the design of equipment to the physiological capacities and needs of the average human organism – indeed it would be impossible to redesign for individual physiological deviations – no such justification exists for psychological qualities. What is at issue in this area is exactly to get away from the assumption of average requirements and take note of individual differences in ability, outlook and life situation. An ergonomic study can be applied directly to the design of equipment. A study of psychological differences yields major distinctions between people that are relevant to the performance of a task. Before they can be applied an intermediate step is required: the assessment of individuals in the available labour force according to the attributes identified by research. The question then arises as to which individual differences should be taken into account in job assignment.

One interesting study demonstrates both the benefits that can be derived from matching job assignment to personal qualities and the difficulty in widespread application because of the high psychological skills required to assess the relevant personality attributes (Morse, 1975). The study dealt with clerical and hourly-paid lower level employees. Based on previous research, jobs were classified according to their degree of routineness or certainty. 'Certain' jobs have rapid feedback on performance, well-defined problems, clear rules, are closely linked to the activities of others; 'uncertain' jobs are the opposite. Four measurable personality attributes predispose an individual to one or the other job type: tolerance of ambiguity, preference for independence from continuously exercised authority, preference for working alone, and ability to deal with complex information. The employees were assigned to jobs that matched their scores on these measures and compared with a group assigned to jobs in the traditional way. About eight months later the employees were tested again for their sense of competence in their jobs and sense of growth and development.

The results showed that those who were fitted to their job, whether it was 'certain' or 'uncertain', much surpassed the traditionally assigned people in their feeling of competence and mastery. These results are encouraging particularly with regard to highly routinised jobs, which apparently need not undermine everybody's morale and development. While the previously quoted Kornhauser (1965) study and Kohn's research (1976; Kohn and Schooler, 1981) suggested that unskilled jobs lead to a deterioration of psychological health, this study implies that this need not be the case if the requirements of the job fit individual predispositions. More than one study is, of course, required to establish the validity of these findings and to discuss whether the personality attributes selected are indeed the most crucial ones; above all it is necessary to develop methods of assessment that are quick and easy to apply on a mass basis. It is not impossible that people's self-assessment of their qualities in four simple choices between opposite pre-dispositions may suffice; but to the best of my knowledge this has not yet been tested. When all this is done, there remains the question of whether or not the number of available jobs in both categories is congruent with the number of the relevant personality attributes in the labour force of a firm, let alone a country. To this question nobody knows the answer, though there is a widespread suspicion that more and more people want challenging jobs while modern technology is assumed by many to lead to the de-skilling of more and more jobs.

In the last century the French utopian socialist Fourier dreamt of a society in which everyone would have the job best suited to him. As he spun out this wonderful dream he arrived at an obstacle: sewer cleaning. Who could possibly be suited to this dirtiest of jobs which was nevertheless essential given the sewage technology of the time? But Fourier was not defeated: he suggested that the task be assigned to ten-year-old boys, whose love for wallowing in dirt he took for granted. Technology has solved this special problem in a different way. The manner in which modern technology will deal with the subtler problems of matching people with tasks remains to be seen.

A mismatch between the demands of a job and the demands of the job-holder exists not only in manual labour on the shopfloor. A recent study of highly trained engineers in industry in their mid-careers, who had graduated from the Massachusetts Institute of Technology between eleven and nineteen years previously (Bailyn, 1980), dis-tinguished three basic orientations to work: a technical orientation, that is people for whom the engineering content of their work is most important; a human orientation, that is people who prefer to work with people rather than with things; and a non-work orientation, that is people for whom family and other concerns are more important than their jobs. Traditionally, however, top positions for engineers in industry are entrepreneurial or managerial, with the result that some technically oriented engineers of high potential either have to change their orientation or remain on lower levels that do not permit them to use fully their technical competence. No wonder that only very few of those who maintain their technical orientation in such positions report high work satisfaction. As with the study quoted before, the application of these findings is confronted with considerable difficulties, but it is not impossible.

Because assessment of individuals for achieving an optimal fit between personal attitudes and a job presents so many technical difficulties, experiments with job enrichment and job enlargement have proceeded either on the assumption that everybody would benefit from greater variety and more autonomy in the performance of their tasks, or occasionally have left participation in such measures open to individual choice where organisational requirements made this possible.

Lisl Klein (1976*b*) has discussed successes and failures with job enrichment in several countries. Sometimes, but not always, these experiments involve participation in decision-making; sometimes, but not always, they affect an entire organisational structure. As she puts it: 'In the long run these change programmes will exert influences of their own and may themselves lead to new institutions, organisational forms, and technologies. They should lead to a greater interpenetration of boundaries between industry and the rest of society, lessening the split between the values expressed in the working arrangements of society and the values expressed in its other institutions' (p. 70).

So we have come full circle: having examined singly the structure of society, the organisational structure of an enterprise and the nature of the tasks as aspects of the humanisation of work without discovering a panacea in any of these three areas, it is suggested by Klein's conclusions that their interaction in a lengthy process of gradual change is required to eliminate, or at least mitigate, the dehumanising features of some forms of employment.

6

Looking back and looking ahead

In the preceding chapters a selection of the findings from empirical research has been presented with the intention of illuminating the psychological meaning of employment and unemployment. It is now appropriate to go beyond the details of documentation to a distillation of the ideas that have emerged and their bearing on current and coming problems and policies.

The structure of employment in the modern world has developed over at least two centuries. While the power of organised labour and changing technologies have significantly influenced this structure, it has remained virtually unaltered in at least two aspects: first, it provides the means whereby the vast majority of people earn their livelihood; and second, as an unintended by-product of its very organisation it enforces on those who participate in it certain categories of experience. These are: it imposes a time structure on the waking day; it enlarges the scope of social relations beyond the often emotionally highly charged family relations and those in the immediate neighbourhood; by virtue of the division of labour it demonstrates that the purposes and achievements of a collectivity transcend those for which an individual can aim; it assigns social status and clarifies personal identity; it requires regular activity.

These enforced categories can be experienced as pleasant or unpleasant; as categories, however, they are inescapable whatever their quality. These categories of experience correspond to more or less deep-seated needs in most people, who strive to make some sense out of their existence. They need to structure their day; they need wider social experiences; they need to partake in collective purposes (and they want the products that result from collective action); they need to know where they stand in society in comparison with others in order to clarify their personal identity; and they need regular activities.

Modern employment is certainly not the only structure in industrialised societies that meets these needs. But it is the dominant one at the moment and the only one that combines the automatic provision of these categories with the overwhelming economic necessity for most people to work for their living.

Whether or not these needs have ultimately a genetic foundation is a question outside my competence to pursue. The fact that there are in non-industrialised societies arrangements to satisfy them that are very different from the structure of modern employment suggests that they are relatively enduring. On the other hand the fact that in industrialised societies families and schools need to exert considerable effort to develop these needs in the young indicates that they cannot be taken for granted as the result of 'natural' maturation. This may suggest the idea that there is nothing fundamental in these needs for experience but that they are imposed on pliable human organisms by the power of prevailing social structures. It is the privilege and obligation of social psychology to avoid the extremes of biological or social determinism by studying the actual interplay between individual needs and available social structures, keeping in mind the possibility that either one may change gradually or suddenly.

Unemployment presents for the individual a sudden change in his or her habitual social structure. What then happens to his or her needs?

Even though social conditions have radically changed for the better during the last half-century, the evidence that is available from then and now suggests that the needs persisted, so that the psychological burden imposed by the absence of the categories of experience that employment provides is comparable in the two periods. During the great depression unemployment implied extreme poverty; at present its tie to absolute deprivation is loosened but relative deprivation is the rule with few, if any, exceptions. In this country it is intensified by the fact that the standard of living of many still in employment has apparently risen over the last few years while unemployment allowances are about to be reduced and some of the free social services provided by the welfare state are being curtailed. Nonetheless the argument that the psychological suffering of the currently unemployed is entirely the result of their economic relative deprivation and could be eliminated by more adequate allowances cannot stand in view of what has been said about the correspondence between the categories of experience provided by employment and human needs. This point is of importance in thinking about future employment levels and I shall return to it. Rejecting the idea that unemployment is a matter of material hardship only is, of course, not equivalent to denying that material hardship is involved; a further deterioration of the standard of living of the unemployed can only add to the burden they already carry.

Different groups of unemployed experience the absence of one category of experience or another with differing intensity. While the missing time structure is apparently a burden for most, it is the young unemployed for whom boredom and not knowing what to do with themselves seem to be the most pressing issues. Unemployed women are most aware of the absence of social contacts, unemployed managers of the lack of status. Depending on a multitude of individual life circumstances and personal qualities conscious experiences must vary, of course. But if the human needs met by employment are indeed as deep-seated and widespread as I assume, and if individuals have not managed to design alternative ways of meeting them, leaving them unmet must have consequences, though the link between the absence of a job and these consequences may escape individual awareness.

From this point of view the studies linking unemployment rates to indicators of social pathology are of importance, though, as has been shown, the controversy over the evidence for this link remains unresolved on the level of methodological technicalities. On the conceptual level the dispute is about whether the absence of categories of experience in unemployment is 'better' or 'worse' than negative experiences within such categories under some conditions of employment. The qualitative differences between these two types of experience make a direct comparison difficult beyond saying that they are both 'bad', each in its own way. The indirect comparison based on correlations between global indicators of social pathology and global economic indicators suffers inevitably from the fact that nobody knows how widespread bad employment conditions are. Unless one maintains (as some do) that all employment is dehumanising, the demonstration that there exists social pathology also under conditions of relatively full employment cannot be taken as proof that bad conditions of employment have worse consequences than unemployment. Judging by what people say, unemployment is subjectively the worse experience. This

85

one infers from the fact that the overwhelming majority of the unemployed want jobs while nobody clamours for unemployment. (At least hardly anybody, though in the heyday of student unrest one group demonstrated for the right to full unemployment.)

It should be noted, however, that while there is some good evidence for assuming that the experience of being unemployed at present has many similarities to that in the thirties, there is as yet no systematic evidence to show that the adaptation to the current experience will be, as it was then, resignation and apathy. This remains one possibility but not the only one. Given a lesser degree of physical deprivation and a higher level of aspiration, it is conceivable that many unemployed as individuals or in groups will make attempts – constructive or destructive – to deal more actively with their frustration.

The experience of frustration is, however, not limited to the unemployed. A sizeable minority of those with jobs are frustrated too, albeit for different reasons and notwithstanding the fact that a large majority declare themselves satisfied with their jobs. Their frustration is due not to the emptiness and lack of experience that accompany being out of work but to the negative quality of their experiences in employment. There is some evidence to show that the negative psychological consequences of some conditions of employment are even more widespread than those concerned realise. For reasons spelled out before it seems unjustified to blame conscious frustration on the demise of the work ethic. People want to work; they need the categories of experience that employment provides; but they need them under conditions that do not diminish their human nature. This does not necessarily imply a rejection of repetitive or dirty or even dangerous jobs; rather it means an employment situation in which individuals have some control over the manner and speed of their activities, understand the reasons for rules and regulations, can make their voices heard and are treated as complete human beings, not as pairs of hands, whatever their specific tasks. Such conditions do exist in some employment, but it is doubtful whether they are the rule. This doubt rests not on the assumption that employers deliberately plan to dehumanise their workforces, but on the lack of evidence that they deliberately plan for humanisation. Dehumanisation is the result of default, not of intent, at least in the vast majority of cases.

Early research findings persuaded some employers that the humanisation of conditions would invariably improve the productivity of the labour force. This was not the case; some industrial experiments with job enrichment or enlargement or with participation in decision-making were discontinued either because they did not meet such expectations or because they were left to the initiative of an individual without being anchored in institutional arrangements within a firm and without involving the trade unions. But some succeeded in improving work satisfaction, management–labour relations, absenteeism, labour turnover and a sense of competence in the workforce. Humanisation efforts undertaken for their own sake rather than for efficiency only need not interfere with efficiency, though they do not automatically increase it. They may sometimes involve some economic costs – their size is hard to estimate and varies with the situation and the adopted means – that must be off-set against the psychological benefit stemming from reducing alienation. These benefits cannot be expressed in financial terms; they accrue to individuals and thereby to society at large, not to a single entrepreneur.

What are the means for appropriate humanisation? There are two overlapping categories: organisational change and changes in the assignment of individuals to specific tasks. Among the former are participation in decision-making on various levels, job enrichment and enlargement, and a variety of co-operative and profit-sharing schemes.

In West Germany participation in decision-making at the top level in large enterprises has become the law of the land, in contrast to this country where similar proposals have not been implemented by legislation. Only a very few enterprises, such as for example the nationalised steel industry, the Post Office or in the private sector the Glacier Metal Company, have comparable arrangements. Neither the economic results nor the psychological consequences for the entire labour force of such arrangements are known with any degree of precision. The difference between West Germany and the U.K. is partly due to the difference in the organisation of trade unions in these two countries: in Germany management can deal with one comprehensive union; here there is a multitude of unions in every large company which are sometimes involved in inter-union disputes.

On the face of it top-level participation will have little influence on the daily work experiences on the shopfloor, unless it serves to safeguard and encourage participatory arrangements on all levels. A growing number – though still small – of U.K. undertakings have some form of participation on the lower levels of the industrial hierarchy. Systematic studies here and elsewhere have indicated that such participation has as a rule psychological consequences that counteract alienation even if they do not increase productivity. But there is one difficulty often found in several countries: those on the lowest, unskilled level who are most in need of an improvement of their work experience in the judgement of researchers and observers want it least and do not readily avail themselves of opportunities if they are offered. Such reluctance to participate is on occasion strengthened by ambivalent attitudes in the trade union movement to such schemes. If looked at in a static fashion this is discouraging; but it should not be forgotten that institutions and people can change, if given a chance. Traditional ideologies and arrangements have taken their toll; it will take deliberate and prolonged efforts on the part of all concerned to break their power.

Where traditional forms of organisation persist while technical processes change, gradually as they often do or radically through the introduction of a completely new technology, the resulting mismatch is often a cause of frustration among employees. Socio-technical systems analysis has demonstrated both the negative effects of such change and the possibility of creating a more appropriate match between social organisation and technology. To be asked to operate under conditions and rules that are no longer suited to the task at hand is an insult to the intelligence of employees whose intimate knowledge of the work processes often remains unused in deference to obsolete forms of organisation. It is, of course, true that there are many manual workers whose knowledge and concern about production processes are very limited, but there are also many who know and care and are hence frustrated, perhaps even driven to no longer caring, if their potential contribution is systematically ignored. Socio-technical systems analysis therefore relies as much on information from the workforce as from management, in contrast to some other managerial 'packages' offered by some social scientists as tools for improvement of efficiency or of labour–management relations, or of both. Where improvements of production procedure and employment conditions are instituted from the top down, such paternalism is hardly likely to produce the desired results with a modern workforce if the workforce's potential intellectual contribution to the technically appropriate organisation of manual labour is by-passed.

Job enrichment and job enlargement – other forms of organisational change designed for the purposes of humanisation – have both successes and failurres to their credit. Their institution can involve considerable organisational change as, for example, in the Swedish motor-car industry; in large-scale office organisations their introduction produces considerably less upheaval and fewer costs and there is much less danger of running into demarcation disputes. As has been indicated before, there is research evidence for the fact that the sense of being underused or inappropriately used in employment is fairly widespread on all levels. With the introduction of new technologies on the shopfloor and in the office many once valuable skills may become obsolete, thus creating additional sources of frustration. Here job enlargement and enrichment could serve as compensatory factors.

Changes in the financial power structure through producer co-operatives and various forms of profit sharing and financial co-ownership, with or without participative arrangements, have the great advantage of tangible results for every individual. There is only very sporadic evidence to show that such arrangements also affect the less tangible psychological factors. Much more should be known about this in a systematic fashion, particularly about those cases where these financial arrangements are combined with other efforts at humanisation. There are, of course, those who argue that only public ownership of the means of production will make humanisation possible; nowhere in the world is there any evidence to prove the point.

The second overlapping category of efforts to humanise employment involves taking note of individual differences by aiming for a proper match between individual predispositions and abilities and assignment to specific tasks. In theory this could be the most effective form of humanisation, for, as has been shown, not everybody wants to participate in decision-making, not everybody wants an enriched or enlarged job. In practice, considerable psychological skill is required to engage in such matching, but the greatest question-mark that hangs over this idea of making everybody contribute according to his or her ability is the assumption that the number and type of available jobs match the distribution of personal qualities among job seekers and holders, nationally or locally. At present, there is some evidence to suggest that on the national level there is a shortage of highly skilled people, an abundance of low skilled. This one infers from the nature of unfilled vacancies and the overrepresentation of unskilled people among the unemployed. Where there is evidence from individual firms, however, the picture looks different; there often seems to be an abundance of people whose skills (albeit not necessarily as formally defined) are underused. The potential of some of the new technologies to further lower the skill level required in many jobs while increasing the need for some highly skilled people threatens to make the difficulty of individual job assignment even greater, at least in a transition period until education and training have caught up with the changing requirements of modern production processes.

Altogether the research evidence leaves little doubt about three facts: (1) there is ample need for humanisation of employment; (2) there are several tested ways of achieving it; but (3) they are likely to fail or be abandoned if undertaken in the wrong expectation that they will also increase productivity. Even where they are introduced, as they should be, for their own sake, they are no instantaneous cure-all. They are beset by difficulties, produce occasional set-backs and require prolonged institutional commitment and personal effort to have an effect. What is more, technological, economic, social and political changes will inevitably modify effects achieved at one moment in time. The humanisation of employment is thus not a goal that can be reached once and for all, but rather a continuing process that needs altering and adapting as people and circumstances change.

The foregoing summary of what emerges from the social-psychological research literature on employment and unemployment has identified major psychological issues that should be taken into consideration when government, trade unions and employers consider industrial strategies, but these are often ignored. As a rule various hotly debated strategies are compared in terms of their assumed economic consequences only. If social psychology is to make a contribution to the public debate about employment levels and their future, there must be clarity about its role among social psychologists: it is a complement to, not a substitute for, other approaches based on systematic thought, notwithstanding the fact that it specifies ends more often than means. Means to such ends will for a long time to come be largely economic, though not exclusively so. But no economic effort will succeed unless it is geared to meeting human needs.

The inevitable limitation of the contribution that social-psychological thought can make is most starkly evidenced by the fact that it has little, if anything, to say on the most important question for the eighties: what level of employment can the economy of the U.K. expect? Even economists, into whose province the issue falls, agree neither on the level nor on the economic policies that could affect that level for better or worse. By and large available estimates are pessimistic and there is much controversy about how to deal with the resulting deprivation of millions of people. Social psychologists are, however, in a somewhat better position to make some informed guesses about the probable social and psychological consequences if mass unemployment is unavoidable in the years ahead.

A distinction must here be made between those who have lost a job and those who never had one, that is the school-leavers who cannot find employment. In this country the number in the latter group has recently been increased by savage cuts in higher and further education. The psychological situation of these 16 to 18 or 19 year old young people to whom the ordinary transition to adulthood is thus denied presents perhaps the socially most dangerous aspect of the current depression. This is the age group on whose skills, motivation to work and general outlook on the world in which they live the future of the country will depend in the next decades. Many of them are without hope, without plans and without ambition and are gradually abandoning the habits and aspirations that family and school had tried to instil in them. And this is true even for those youngsters who were made redundant in the middle of an apprenticeship or held for a few weeks odd, unrewarding jobs. Dan van der Vat (1981) has recently documented in three brilliant articles, based on conversations with young people and on some survey data, the plight of this generation. Many have not lost their will to work, at least not yet; many others have. Whether or not they will recover their ability to live within adult society if and when the chance comes is a moot question.

Where unemployment lasts longer than a few weeks those who have lost their jobs have to deal in one form or another with the painful experience that some of the psychological needs they share with the employed and which are deeply anchored in the social norms of this society are no longer automatically met by current institutional arrangements. Several types of response to this ineluctable situation may occur: the unemployed may maintain their needs and may take out their resulting frustration on themselves or their families; they may gradually adapt to unemployment by relinquishing their needs; they may create or find alternative arrangements that meet their needs; they may revolt against their fate in organised fashion; they may engage in sporadic outbursts venting their frustration and accumulated diffuse hostility in riots and looting. At different times of their experience of unemployment individuals may engage in two or more of these responses.

The first type is psychologically destructive and socially particularly damaging because it may be most frequent among people who were most involved with their jobs. If repeated job applications remain unsuccessful self-confidence may well be undermined. Depending on a person's tolerance for frustration, mental breakdown or even suicides could follow. The fact that only a few such cases are known so far, makes one hope that they actually are infrequent. More often, the experience of prolonged frustration translates into withdrawal from social contacts, bad temper and moodiness, all of them damaging to marital relations and the upbringing of children.

Adjustment to unemployment by giving up, appears to have been the dominant response in the thirties. In this category now are the apathetic and discouraged unemployed who no longer search for jobs. They have adjusted to living somehow on their meagre allowances. For a man or a woman with a young family this may not be an easy stance to take, but it is a possible one. It is easier for single people, some of whom have even come to like their welfare-supported existence, and have not only given up their search for jobs but even their willingness to enter employment. There are reasonably well documented examples of such opting out, perhaps particularly among the educated young. It is easy to blame students who after having got a degree settle down quite happily for a time to living on welfare, but it would be wrong to assume that more than a handful can manage such a life psychologically for any length of time. The unmet needs take their toll, and the likelihood of people trying to forget them by participation in the drug culture is as high as the likelihood that they will switch to another type of response to their life situation.

92

The social consequences of having a large number of unemployed people who have somehow managed to kill their own deep-seated psychological needs are particularly serious when such unemployed are heads of families. Having relinquished one's own needs for time structure, status and identity, a social purpose, social experience and regular activity is hardly a promising condition for developing these needs in children. These needs are developed gradually within the family if the parents live within the norms of the larger society. If they do not but have accepted their role as outcasts through prolonged unemployment this is what will be transmitted to their young as a model to emulate. Being on time at school, going to school at all, may appear hardly worth the effort; making plans for the future will not be encouraged in an atmosphere of hopelessness. It has become fashionable to blame parents for the misbehaviour of their young, even to punish them for it. Neither blame nor punishment will have any constructive impact on people demoralised by long-term unemployment.

The invention or discovery of alternative arrangements through which the needs frustrated by lack of employment can be met has constructive and destructive aspects. Some of the unemployed, sometimes supported by employed people, are trying to create new forms of working collectively that, much as traditional employment, combine the good reason of making a living with the psychological benefits that such arrangements provide. A group of Welsh unemployed with the support of their union went to Mondragon in Spain to learn how to establish a producer co-operative. In other parts of the country similar attempts are being made, particularly by those like the steel-workers who received relatively high redundancy payments that they were willing to invest in a common enterprise. No systematic information on the success or failure of such efforts seems to be available. Sporadic information is more specific on the failures than the successes which surely must also exist. Not enough capital, lack of managerial and marketing experience together with the general recession appear to be the main causes of failure. If, when and where such efforts succeed they would not only present the most constructive response to unemployment but also provide an opportunity for the humanisation of conditions. The danger of such current enterprises lies in the fact that they are more often than not made in traditional industries in which

93

competition from abroad is particularly strong. Psychologically they testify to the persisting will to work of those involved. They deserve much more advice and support from unions, experienced managers and government than they apparently receive. Similar psychological benefits and difficulties arise in the efforts of some who are stimulated by their experience of unemployment to attempt to become self-employed by turning an invention, idea or a hobby into a saleable product, becoming shopkeepers or hawkers. All too little is known about their numbers, successes or failures.

The communes established by some people, mostly the young and not exclusively manned by the unemployed, are another constructive alternative to traditional forms of employment. They are as a rule built on idealism and hard work but have usually a short life expectancy for good psychological reasons: they are not a way into the larger society but a way out of it. Many who enter a commune with high hopes begin to feel claustrophobic after a while, recognise it as a temporary escape rather than a permanent solution, and leave. There also exists a pernicious form of such communes, often in pseudo-religious guise, where the idealism or the despair of the entrants is shamelessly exploited by those in charge.

Work not in order to earn a living is for some, for some length of time, an appropriate alternative to employment if they can manage to live within their financial support from public funds or belong to the lucky few who have private means. In both cases, however, such work lacks the compelling aspect of employment in providing the necessary categories of experience and hence depends on a degree of personal initiative that is rare among all strata of the population, but perhaps particularly so among those who form the bulk of the unemployed – the unskilled and the young.

The psychological burden of unemployment is perhaps least among those women to whom the alternative of returning to the traditional role of housewife is open, but there are many to whom it is not and many others for whom it is very much a second best. Nonetheless the argument is sometimes made that the unemployment rate could be significantly reduced if married women were excluded from the labour force. Even apart from the cultural regression this would imply, it is extremely doubtful that unemployed men could or would fill the vacancies so created in school teaching, nursing, clerical and secretarial work and other still 'female' occupations. The very great number of housewives who need tranquillisers to get through the day or turn to drink testifies to the stress many experience in this role. Their number may well be further increased by women who had experienced the satisfaction that employment provides before the loss of their jobs compelled them to return to their traditional role.

There are also destructive ways of meeting the needs that used to be met by employment. Perhaps economically most damaging is the spread of participation in the black economy, though it is not known to what extent it is a side-line activity for those in regular employment or an alternative to unemployment. Whichever is the case in that respect, it must be recognised that it is from a psychological perspective a complete alternative, even implying the bonus of greater independence and more self-regulation than is available in legal employment, unless it is organised on an exploitative pattern when that bonus is limited, of course, to the unofficial boss only. If the black economy were to become a major alternative to unemployment it would present most serious moral, social and economic problems. Because of the economic and psychological advantages to individuals of this social threat its elimination is both immensely difficult and strongly indicated.

On a smaller scale organised crime shares the psychological benefits of the black economy; while its consequences are even more obviously damaging, like the black economy it is not caused by unemployment though it may be augmented by it. In sharp contrast to the thirties, nowhere do the unemployed seem to regard begging as a tolerable alternative to employment.

A third possible response to prolonged unemployment is violent and organised revolt, if not revolution, under the leadership of the extreme right or the extreme left. Political groups of both kinds exist and are undoubtedly trying to use the frustration of the unemployed for their purposes. (In the current political climate that is rich in invective it is perhaps not unnecessary to be explicit: I do not mean the leaders of the current government nor of the left-wing of the Labour Party. Though they are occasionally described as extreme right or left neither plans violent revolt.) It lies in the nature of these mostly clandestine groups that it is impossible to say whether the unemployed have joined them in significant numbers. As far as one can judge from studies of the unemployed – as much as from voting research and behaviour – rather

95

the opposite is the case. What the unemployed want most is a job, not revolution. The relative social isolation that their condition often implies heightens individualistic concerns. The growing gap between their standard of living and that of most still in employment is not conducive to creating a sense of solidarity with a nationwide social class or social purpose.

And yet, the possibility of organised violent revolt using the unemployed cannot be denied. The danger is greater from the extreme right than the extreme left for two reasons. First, because the extreme right in their violent actions and racist propaganda put the blame for the country's economic plight on the presence of immigrants and their children. However misleading and simple-minded this is as an explanation for mass unemployment, it has a surface plausibility that may find an echo in the minds of some unemployed. Second, the quasi-military authoritarian form of organisation into which such groups try to lure young unemployed meets several of the needs frustrated by lack of a job. Ideological commitments on the extreme left, on the other hand, preclude at least an appeal to racial discrimination. For all one knows their secret organisations may offer attractions similar to those of the extreme right, but they apparently aim at a highly selective, not mass, recruitment.

The fourth type of response is the periodic outbreak of rioting and looting as a temporary relief from material and psychological frustration. Recent riots in England's inner cities have been widely attributed to unemployment. But rioting is certainly not restricted to the unemployed, nor is it new in the history of this country or elsewhere. The youth riots in Switzerland occurred during full employment; rioting at football matches is an all too frequent occurrence; and year in year out television carries the excitement of rioting and the knowledge of how to do it into virtually every home with pictures of the tragedy of Ulster. Such riots are quite different from organised revolt even if some extreme groups try to exploit them for their purposes. The characteristics of recent rioting were: the age of the participants (school-children and young people); the lack – in most cases, not in all – of any social purpose; and their location in the inner cities where deprivation of many kinds was the rule even before mass unemployment became a major issue.

Rioting for a night or two certainly brings psychological relief for the time of its duration, at least from inactivity and boredom. But, like other forms of delinquency it is not just the result of unemployment though it may appeal particularly to young unemployed people. Even though most adult unemployed show at present little inclination to join in riots and are probably as horrified as the rest of the population by the human damage and material losses they cause, there is a frightening logic to rioting that will not escape their notice: riots produce results. No government could ignore rioting on the scale that recently shook England's inner cities. Although the plight of the inner cities had long been documented and was widely known, only the riots seemed to produce some action. In addition to the arrest and indictment of some of those involved action began to be taken to deal with some of the reasons for the frustration that had exploded. If public policy is rigidly limited to economic considerations and ignores the psychological and material burden imposed on parts of the population, the most energetic and least responsible among them will demonstrate that only violent rioting will bring some public recognition of the circumstances under which they live.

What one would like to know is which of these types of response to unemployment will dominate in this decade. There is, of course, no hard and fast answer beyond saying that some of each will be in evidence. Much depends on the policies that will govern economic development and on social policies that influence the distribution among groups of the population of the economic hardship that is undoubtedly ahead. Within these limitations I can only offer a personal guess.

It seems to me that most of the unemployed will after the first two months or so take out their frustration for a limited time on themselves or their families or both. This may well, however, remain a lasting response for many, particularly perhaps those who were involved with their jobs; having experienced genuine satisfaction in their previous employment nothing but the restoration of the *status quo* may appear to them worthwhile. If that *status quo* fails to materialise, frustration may accumulate beyond a tolerable level, and explode – depending on personality predisposition – into self-punishment or other punishing acts. On the other hand people who were involved with their work will find the transition back into employment easier than will others, if the opportunity for it arises in time.

Employment and unemployment

Resignation and apathy as the result of suppressing one's needs will be less dominant among the unemployed of the eighties than it was among those of the thirties, even though it will still be the response of many. Giving up comes less automatically to people in better health, with a higher standard of living, and a higher level of education and aspiration than was the case then. There may well be an age difference here, with a majority of the unemployed aged 50 and above taking this stance.

The search for alternatives to meet deep-seated human needs may well be more extensive than it was in the past. This guess is based in part also on the higher level of aspiration and in addition on much evidence that the will to work has not disappeared among a large majority of the unemployed. The question is whether these alternatives will be on the socially constructive or destructive side. As long as the world recession lasts the various constructive alternatives cannot easily come to fruition, and certainly not unless they are supported financially by public or trade union funds. There is hence a likelihood that the black economy and organised crime of minor and major scope will continue to grow.

Revolutionary responses to the situation are least likely. I infer their low probability from the dominance of personal not social concerns among the unemployed and from the absence of any tangible solidarity between the employed and the unemployed. If organised violent revolt were to occur, it is most unlikely that the initiative would come from among the unemployed, but the possibility of their being exploited by extremists cannot be totally excluded.

Sporadic rioting and looting will probably not disappear from the social scene and may well increase in frequency, particularly if riots remain the only means of producing visible results in the deprived areas of the country. The demoralising effects of repeated riots on the entire population, in whom they create physical fear and antagonism to the young and particularly to young blacks, is in the long run probably quite as harmful as the actual damage done.

This is not a hopeful set of expectations for the next few years, but rosy prediction would have to ignore stark realities. There is an apparently simple solution to mass unemployment: the shortening of working hours by 10, 15 or 20%. For several reasons such simplicity is more apparent than real. Given the comparatively low level of British wages and salaries, organised labour would not and could not accept wage cuts by the same proportion. Any attempt to create employment for all by such cuts might create social upheaval on a scale larger than that of the riots. To pay the same wages for significantly reduced hours to a larger workforce, however, would lower British competitiveness on the world market even further. But even if the world market could absorb more expensive goods – an unlikely assumption anyhow – the attempt could not succeed because of the geographical distribution of unemployment and the mismatch between the skills of the unemployed and the skills required by modern enterprises.

And yet, in the long run the shortening of working hours per day, per year or per life-time is the most constructive measure if new technologies actually reduce the amount of work required to give the population a respectable standard of living. The psychological benefits of employment are not tied to an eight-hour day or a forty-hour week. They would accrue even in the inprobable case for this century that working hours could be halved without lowering the standard of living. In this country as elsewhere a gradual reduction of working hours is actually taking place and there are efforts afoot to cut overtime, one of the few positive aspects of an otherwise dark picture. The immediate impact of such developments will be mostly an improvement in the quality of working life for the employed; it is inevitably a slow way of reducing the number of the unemployed.

While the reduction of working hours is in the long run a clear link to controlling unemployment, in the short run it will have little effect. This does, of course, not diminish the importance of improving the quality of working life now. The large majority of the population will remain in employment well beyond the next decades. The more satisfying their experiences are, the less is the chance that they will lose their will to work should unemployment hit them. That much can be done in that respect has been documented in earlier pages, even though this too will be a slow process. To the difficulties confronting humanisation of work mentioned before will be added the problems that may arise from the introduction of new and advanced technologies that should preoccupy trade unions and employers beyond their possible impact on employment levels.

It is generally agreed that if and when British enterprises catch up with these technologies they will require a labour force that is capable of continuing learning throughout a life-time and is flexible in the exercise of a variety of skills, both high and low, in a variety of jobs. The idea of one job only during a working life has already become obsolete. The extent to which the current content and organisation of school education is suited to helping young people to develop these qualities is doubtful. A discussion of the contribution of school education to the future quality of working life is outside the scope of this book, beyond saying that the traditional idea that education stops at a given age, that adults work or are unemployed but do not participate in education while children learn, is out of date; the current strict separation of age groups, institutionalised in the school system, may well be a contributory factor to the frequency of conflicts between the young and adults.

More to the point of the present discussion is the question of what employers and trade unions could do to increase the flexibility of the labour force. The extension of training and education is obviously required, and the example of West Germany in this respect is often quoted. Beyond these requirements, however, other things must change too. The current organisation of employment incorporates rigidities in most cases that impinge on the immediate experience of the labour force and make demands for flexibility just words, not a living reality to be emulated. In attitude and behaviour trade unions and employers alike encourage a strict limitation of jobs and responsibilities, jealously guarding demarcation lines. The very principle of organisation of British unions impedes the possibility of changing jobs or skills or using a variety of skills within the same job. Employers more often than not maintain a strict hierarchy, emphasised by many real or symbolic 'do's and 'don't's for every level of the organisation, from eating and toilet facilities to working hours and extent of holidays. Attitudes and organisational principles are notoriously hard to change, but since we all respond more readily to direct experience than to exhortation, unless they do change the necessary flexibility in the labour force will be slow to emerge. These matters are urgent in the current situation, but there is little sign that they will be tackled within this decade.

The near future presents other problems in employment and unemployment that go beyond the competence of social psychologists to document, let alone resolve. And yet social psychologists must be heard in the public debate for they have a contribution to make that those who have to worry about inflation, trade balances, productivity and other economic issues all too often tend to forget: the systematic demonstration that people matter.

References

Bailyn, L. (1980). *Living with Technology: Issues at Mid-Career.* Cambridge, Mass., and London: M.I.T. Press.

Bakke, E. W. (1933). *The Unemployed Man.* London: Nisbet.

Banks, M. H., Clegg, C. W., Jackson, P. R., Kemp, N. J., Stafford, E. M. and Wall, T. D. (1980). The use of the General Health Questionnaire as an indicator of mental health in occupational studies. *Journal of Occupational Psychology*, **53**, 187–94.

Banks, O. (1960). *The Attitudes of Steelworkers to Technical Change.* Liverpool University Press.

Baumgartner, T., Burns, T. R. and Seculic, D. (1979). Self-management, market and political institutions in conflict: Yugoslav development patterns and dialectics. In *Work and Power*, ed. T. R. Burns, L. E. Karlsson and U. Rus. London: Sage Publications.

Binyon, M. (1981). The Russian who advocates unemployment. *The Times*, 20 January, p.19.

Brake, T. (1978). *Work Organisation: A Bibliography 1970–77.* Compiled for the Social Science Research Council, School Government Company Ltd.

Brenner, M. H. (1976). *Estimating the Social Costs of National Economic Policy: Implications for Mental and Physical Health, and Criminal Aggression.* Joint Economic Committee of Congress, Paper No. 5. Washington, D.C.: U.S. Government Printing Office.

Brewer, G. (1975). *Workers Without Jobs.* Australia: Brotherhood of St Lawrence.

Brinkmann, C. (1981). Finanzielle und psycho-soziale Belastungen während der Arbeitslosigkeit. In *Vom Schock zum Fatalismus?*, ed. A. Wacker. Frankfurt: Campus Verlag.

Brittan, S. (1981). The cost of employing the unemployed. *Financial Times*, 15 January.

Brown, G. (1977). *Sabotage: A Study in Industrial Conflict.* Nottingham: Spokesman Books.

102

Brown, J. A. C. (1954). *The Social Psychology of Industry*. London: Penguin Books.

Bullock, Lord (1977). *Report of the Committee of Inquiry on Industrial Democracy*. London: H.M.S.O.

Casson, M. (1979). *Youth Unemployment*. London: Macmillan.

Catalano, R. and Dooley, C. D. (1977). The economic predictors of depressed mood and stressful life events in a metropolitan community. *Journal of Health and Social Behaviour*, **18**(3), 292–307.

Coch, L. and French, J. P. R. Jr (1948). Overcoming resistance to change. *Human Relations*, **1**(4), 512–32.

Council of Social Service of N.S.W. (1978). *Unemployed Women*. Council of Social Service of New South Wales.

Davis, L.E. (1977). Evolving alternative organisation designs: their socio-technical bases. *Human Relations*, **30**(3), 261–73.

den Hertog, F. J. (1976). Workstructuring. In *Personal Goals and Work Design*, ed. P. Warr. New York: Wiley.

D.H.E.W. (1973). *Work in America*. Department of Health, Education and Welfare. Cambridge, Mass.: M.I.T. Press.

Dunlop, J. T. (1978). Past and future tendencies in American labour organisations. *Daedalus*, Winter, 79–96.

Eisenberg, P. and Lazarsfeld, P. F. (1938). The psychological effects of unemployment. *Psychological Bulletin*, **35**, 358–90.

Elliot, J. (1978). *Conflict or Co-operation? The Growth of Industrial Democracy*. London: Kogan Page.

European Omnibus (1978). *Chômage et recherche d'un emploi: attitudes et opinions des publics Européens*. Brussels: European Communities Commission.

Evan, W. M. (1977). Hierarchy, alienation, commitment and organizational design. *Human Relations*, **30**(1), 77–94.

Eyer, J. (1977*a*). Prosperity as a cause of death. *International Journal of Health Services*, **7**(1), 125–49.

Eyer, J. (1977*b*). Does unemployment cause the death rate peak in each business cycle? *International Journal of Health Services*, **7**(4), 625–62.

Fineman, S. (1979). A psychological model of stress and its application to managerial unemployment. *Human Relations*, **32**(4), 323–43.

Freud, S. (1930). *Civilisation and its Discontents*. Standard edn, vol. 21. London: Hogarth (1963).

Gardner, G. (1977). Workers' participation. A critical evaluation of Coch and French. *Human Relations*, **30**(12), 1071–8.

Garraty, J. A. (1978). *Unemployment in History, Economic Thought and Public Policy*. New York: Harper.

103

References

Gatti, A. (1937). La disoccupazione come crisi psychologica. Quoted in P. Eisenberg and P. F. Lazarsfeld (1938). The psychological effects of unemployment. *Psychological Bulletin*, **35**, 358–90.

Ginzberg, M. (1980). Youth unemployment. *Scientific American*, **242**(5), 31–7.

Guest, R. H. (1952). *The Man on the Assembly Line*. Cambridge, Mass.: Harvard University Press.

Gurney, M. (1980). The effects of unemployment on the psycho-social development of school-leavers. *Occupational Psychology*, **53**, 205–13.

Hallgren, M. A. (1933). *Seeds of Revolt*. Quoted in P. Eisenberg and P. F. Lazarsfeld (1938). The psychological effects of unemployment. *Psychological Bulletin*, **35**, 358–90.

Haraszti, M. (1977). *A Worker in a Workers' State*. Harmondsworth, Middx: Penguin.

Hartley, J. (1980). The impact of unemployment upon the self esteem of managers. *Journal of Occupational Psychology*, **53**, 147–55.

Hartmann, H. (1964). Notes on the reality principle. In *Essays on Ego Psychology*. New York: International Universities Press.

Hawkins, K. (1979). *Unemployment*. Harmondsworth, Middx: Penguin.

Hawrylyshyn, O. (1971). *Estimating the Value of Household Work in Canada*. Ottawa: Statistics Canada.

Hebb, D. and Thompson, W. R. (1954). The social significance of animal studies. In *Handbook of Social Psychology*, ed. G. Lindsey, vol. 1. London and New York: Addison Wesley.

Heinemann, K. (1978). *Arbeitslose Jugendliche*. Darmstadt: Luchterhand.

Heinemann, K., Röhrig, P. and Stadie, R. (1980). *Arbeitslose Frauen im Spannungsfeld von Erwerbstätigkeit und Hausfrauenrolle* (2 vols.). Melle: Ernst Knoll.

Hill, M. J. (1978). The psychological impact of unemployment. *New Society*, 19 January, 118–20.

Hirsch, F. (1977). *The Social Limits to Growth*. London: Routledge and Kegan Paul.

Hofstede, G. (1979). Humanisation of work: the role of values in a third industrial revolution. In *The Quality of Working Life in Western and Eastern Europe*, ed. C. L. Cooper and E. Mumford. London: Associated Business Press.

Hopwood, A. (1979). Toward the economic assessment of new forms of work organisation. In *The Quality of Working Life in Western and Eastern Europe*, ed. C. L. Cooper and E. Mumford. London: Associated Business Press.

Hyman, H. H. (1979). The effects of unemployment: a neglected problem in modern social research. In *Qualitative and Quantitative Social Research: Papers in Honour of Paul F. Lazarsfeld*, ed. R. K. Merton *et al*. New York: Free Press.

Jahoda, M. (1938). Unemployed men at work. Unpublished manuscript.

Jahoda, M. (1979). Toward a participatory society? *New University Quarterly*, Spring, 204–19.

Jahoda, M. (1981). Work, employment and unemployment: values, theories and approaches in social research. *American Psychologist*, **36**(2), 184–91.

Jahoda, M., Lazarsfeld, P. F. and Zeisel, H. (1933). *Marienthal: The Sociography of an Unemployed Community*. (English translation 1972.) London: Tavistock Publications.

Jenkins, C. and Sherman, B. (1979). *The Collapse of Work*. London: Eyre Methuen.

Kanter, R. M. (1978). Work in a new America. *Daedalus*, **107**(1), Winter, 47–78.

Kasl, S. V. (1979). Changes in mental health status associated with job loss and retirement. In *Stress and Mental Disorder*, ed. J. Barret *et al*. New York: Raven Press.

Katz, R. and Van Maanen, J. (1977). The loci of work satisfaction: job interaction and policy. *Human Relations*, **30**(5), 469–86.

Kelvin, P. (1980). Social psychology 2001: the social psychological implications of structural unemployment. In *The Development of Social Psychology*, ed. R. Gilmore and S. Duck. London: Academic Press.

Klein, L. (1964). *Multiproducts Ltd*. London: H.M.S.O.

Klein, L. (1976a). *A Social Scientist in Industry*. London: Gower Press.

Klein, L. (1976b). *New Forms of Work Organisation*. Cambridge University Press.

Kluckhohn, C., Murray, H. A. and Schneider, D. M. (eds.) (1955). *Personality in Nature, Society and Culture*. New York: Knopf.

Kohn, M. L. (1976). Occupational structure and alienation. *American Journal of Sociology*, **82**(1), 111–31.

Kohn, M. L. and Schooler, C. (1981). The reciprocal effects of the substantive complexity of work and intellectual flexibility: a longitudinal assessment. *American Journal of Sociology*, **84**(1), 24–52.

Kornhauser, A. (1965). *Mental Health of the Industrial Worker*. New York: Wiley.

Kuleshova, L. M. and Mamontova, T. I. (1979). Sotsiologicheskie Issledovaniya, No. 2. In: Part-time working. *New Society*, 30 August.

Kumar, K. (1978). *Prophecy and Progress*. London: Allen Lane.

References

Kurczewski, J. (1981). System Krise in Poland. *Journal für Sozialforschung*, **21**(1), 53–68.

Lancet (1979). Editorial: Does unemployment kill? *Lancet*, 31 March. See also letters on pp. 498, 558, 672, 780, 923–4, and 1189.

Landsberger, H. A. (1958). *Hawthorne Revisited*. Cornell Studies in Industrial and Labour Relations. Ithaca, New York.

Leithäuser, T. (1979). Die subjektive Relevanz der Arbeit in krisenhaften sozialen Situationen. University of Bremen (mimeo).

Linhart, R. (1976). *L'Etabli*. Paris: Editions de Minuet.

Lischeron, J. A. and Wall, T. D. (1975). Employee participation: an experimental field study. *Human Relations*, **28**(9), 863–84.

Long, R. J. (1978). The effects of employee ownership on organisational identification, employee job attitudes, and organisational performance: a tentative framework and empirical findings. *Human Relations*, **31**(1), 29–48.

Lüdtke, A. (1979). The role of state violence in the period of transition to industrial capitalism: the example of Russia 1815–1848. *Social History*, **4**(2).

Lupton, T. (1963). *On the Shop Floor*. London: Pergamon Press.

McLoughlin, J. (1980). Two to a job. *The Guardian*, 27 May.

Marsden, D. and Duff, E. (1975). *Workless*. Harmondsworth, Middx: Penguin.

Maslow, A. H. (1970). *Motivation and Personality*, 2nd edn. New York: Harper.

Maurer, H. (1979). *Not Working: An Oral History of the Unemployed*. New York: Holt, Rinehart and Winston.

Mayo, E. (1945). *The Social Problems of an Industrial Civilisation*. Boston, Mass.: Graduate School of Business Administration, Harvard University.

Meissner, M. (1971). The long arm of the job: a study of work and leisure. *Industrial Relations*, **10**, 239–60.

Miller, E. J. (1975). Socio-technical systems in weaving, 1953–1970: a follow-up study. *Human Relations*, **28**(4), 349–86.

Morse, J. T. (1975). Person–job congruence and individual adjustment and development. *Human Relations*, **28**(9), 841–61.

Mozina, S., Jerovsek, J., Tannenbaum, A. S. and Likert, R. (1976). Testing a management style. In *Participative Management: Concepts, Theory and Implementation*, ed. E. Williams. Atlanta, Georgia: Public Services School of Business Administration.

Nathanson, C. A. (1980). Social roles and health status among women: the significance of employment. *Social Science and Medicine*, **14A**(6), 463–72.

106

Orpen, C. (1979). The effects of job enrichment on employee satisfaction, motivation, involvement and performance: a field experiment. *Human Relations*, **32**(3), 189–217.

Palm, G. (1977). *The Flight from Work*. Cambridge University Press.

Pfeffer, R. M. (1979). *Working for Capitalism*. New York: Columbia University Press.

Powell, R. M. and Schlacter, J. L. (1976). Participative management: a panacea? In *Participative Management: Concepts, Theory and Implementation*, ed. E. Williams. Atlanta, Georgia: Public Services School of Business Administration.

Pym, D. (1975). The demise of management and the ritual of employment. *Human Relations*, **28**(8), 675–98.

Pym, D. (1980). Towards the dual economy and emancipation from employment. *Futures*, **12**(3), 223–37.

Rice, A. K. (1958). *Productivity and Social Organisation: The Ahmedabad Experiment*. London: Tavistock Publications.

Roethlisberger, F. J. and Dickson, W. J. (1939). *Management and the Worker*. Cambridge, Mass.: Harvard University Press.

Sahlins, M. (1974). *Stone Age Economics*. London: Tavistock.

Save the Children International Union (1933). *Children, Young People and Unemployment*. Geneva.

Schlesinger, A. (1978). *Robert Kennedy and His Times*. Boston, Mass.: Houghton Mifflin.

Showler, B. (1981). Political economy and unemployment. In *The Workless State*, ed. B. Showler and A. Sinfield. Oxford: Martin Robertson.

Showler, B. and Sinfield, A. (eds.) (1981). *The Workless State*. Oxford: Martin Robertson.

Smith, A. (1776/1937). *Wealth of Nations*. London: Cannon.

Smith, D. J. (1976). *The Facts of Racial Disadvantage*. London: P.E.P.

Smith, D. J. (1981). *Unemployment and Racial Minorities*. London: Policy Studies Institute.

Social Trends (1980). London: H.M.S.O.

Sorrentino, C. (1979). *International Comparisons of Unemployment*. U.S.A. Bureau of Labor Statistics Bulletin.

Stiefel, D. (1979). *Arbeitslosigkeit: Am Beispiel Österreichs, 1918–1938*. Berlin: Duncker and Humbolt.

Stokes, G. (1981). Unemployment among school-leavers. University of Birmingham (mimeo).

Swimburne, P. (1981). The psychological impact of unemployment on managers and professional staff. *Journal of Occupational Psychology*, **54**, 47–64.

References

Sydenstone, E. (1936). Surgeon General's report on health and depression study. *Milbank Memorial Fund Quarterly*, vol. XIV (July), pp. 205–8.

Temmen, H. (1979). Zur Gestaltung 'progressiver Arbeitsinhalte' in der industriellen Produktion: das Beispiel der Montagefliessbänder. *Sozialwissenschaftliche Informationen, Unterricht und Studium*, **8**(4).

Tizard, J. and Anderson, E. (1979). *The Education of the Handicapped Adolescent.* Paris: O.E.C.D.

Trist, L. and Bamford, K. W. (1951). Some social and psychological consequences of the longwall method of coalgetting. *Human Relations*, **4**(4), 3–38.

van der Vat, D. (1981). The plight of Britain's youth. *The Times*, 6 October, p. 6; 8 October, p. 11; 9 October, p. 10.

Wacker, A. (ed.) (1981). *Vom Schock zum Fatalismus?* Frankfurt: Campus Verlag.

Westley, W. A. (1979). Problems and solutions in the quality of working life. *Human Relations*, **32**(2), 113–23

William Temple Foundation (1980). The best years of their lives: work and unemployment in Oldfield. Manchester Business School (mimeo).

Williams, E. (ed.) (1976). *Participative Management: Concepts, Theory and Implementation.* Atlanta, Georgia: Public Services School of Business Administration.

Willis, P. E. (1977). *Learning to Labour.* Farnborough, Hants.: Saxon House.

Winter, J. M. (1981). Economic instability and infant mortality in England and Wales, 1920–1950. Pembroke College, Cambridge (mimeo).

Wood, J. B. (1981). How little unemployment? Quoted in B. Showler and A. Sinfield (eds.) *The Workless State*, p. 46. Oxford: Martin Robertson.

Woodward, J. (1965). *Industrial Organisation: Theory and Practice.* London: Oxford University Press.

Zawadski, B. and Lazarsfeld, P. F. (1935). The psychological consequences of unemployment. *Journal of Social Psychology*, **6**, 224–51.

Name index

Name index

Subject index

Subject index